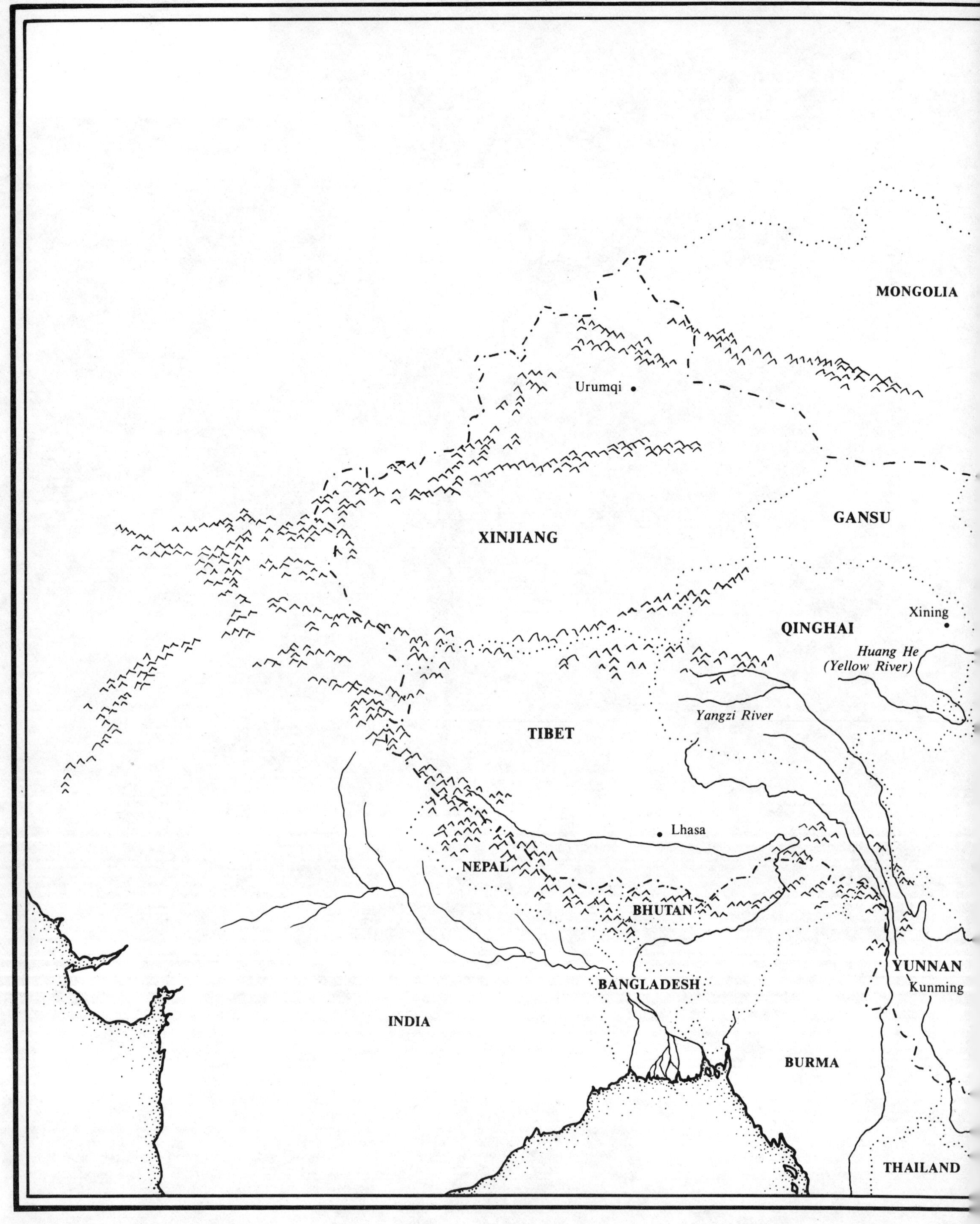

MONGOLIA
Urumqi
GANSU
XINJIANG
QINGHAI
Xining
Huang He
(Yellow River)
Yangzi River
TIBET
Lhasa
NEPAL
BHUTAN
YUNNAN
Kunming
BANGLADESH
INDIA
BURMA
THAILAND

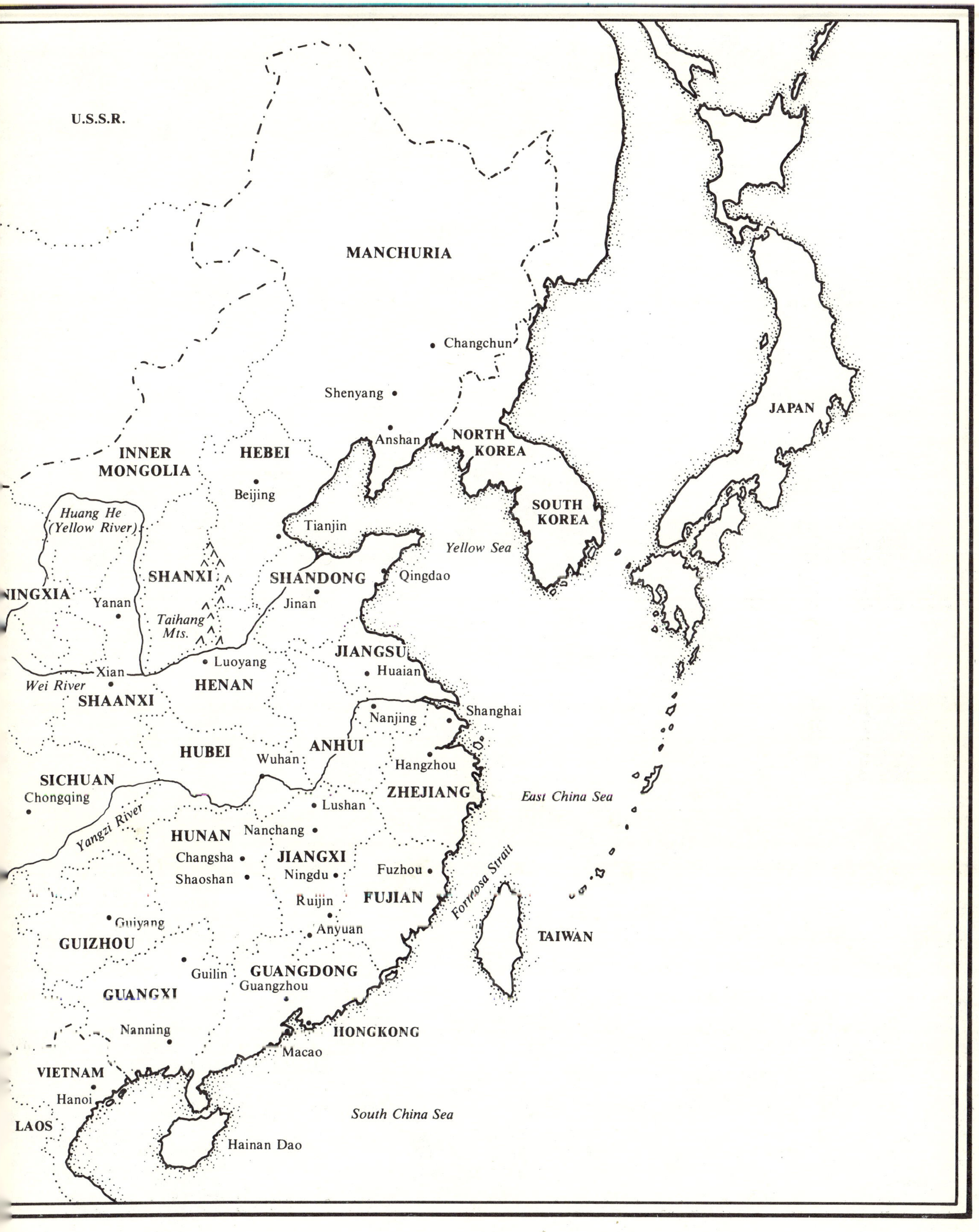

U.S.S.R.
MANCHURIA
Changchun
Shenyang
Anshan
NORTH KOREA
JAPAN
SOUTH KOREA
INNER MONGOLIA
HEBEI
Beijing
Huang He (Yellow River)
Tianjin
Yellow Sea
SHANXI
SHANDONG
Qingdao
NINGXIA
Yanan
Jinan
Taihang Mts.
JIANGSU
Xian
Luoyang
Huaian
Wei River
HENAN
SHAANXI
Nanjing
Shanghai
HUBEI
ANHUI
Wuhan
Hangzhou
SICHUAN
ZHEJIANG
East China Sea
Chongqing
Lushan
Yangzi River
HUNAN
Nanchang
Changsha
JIANGXI
Shaoshan
Ningdu
Fuzhou
Ruijin
FUJIAN
Formosa Strait
Guiyang
Anyuan
TAIWAN
GUIZHOU
Guilin
GUANGDONG
Guangzhou
GUANGXI
Nanning
HONGKONG
Macao
VIETNAM
Hanoi
LAOS
South China Sea
Hainan Dao

# Coming of Grace

# Coming of Grace

## An Illustrated Biography of

# Zhou Enlai

## by Ed Hammond

LANCASTER–MILLER PUBLISHERS/ASIAN HUMANITIES PRESS

Berkeley, California 1980

Copyright ©1980 LANCASTER–MILLER, INC.
3165 Adeline Street
Berkeley, California 94703



Book designed by Carol Egenolf with Jane Bernard, cover based
on a design by Myland McRevey, cover mechanicals prepared
by Fifth Street Design Associates, maps by Jane Bernard,
production by Gail Tsukiyama, George Kelly and Don Petersen.

Cloth: ISBN 0-89581-455-2
Paper: ISBN 0-89591-503-6

**Library of Congress Cataloging in Publication Data**
Hammond, Ed, 1945-
Coming of grace.

Bibliography: p.
1. Chou, En-lai, 1898-1976. 2. Prime ministers—
China—Biography. I. Title.
DS778.C593H35      951.05'092'4  [B]  80-82393
ISBN O-89581-455-2
ISBN O-89581-503-6 (pbk.)

*For all of my family*

# A NOTE ON PRONUNCIATION

This book uses the international system adopted in 1979 for transcribing Chinese characters. The only exceptions are for Chiang Kaishek and Sun Yatsen, two well-known figures whose names historically have been pronounced in southern Chinese dialects and as such are not susceptible to standardized transcription.

The following is the Pinyin system's alphabet with American English equivalents.

| | |
|---|---|
| *a* | as in *far* |
| *ao* | as in *cow* |
| *b* | as in *be* |
| *c* | as in *its* |
| *ch* | as in *church* |
| *d* | as in *do* |
| *e* | as in *her* |
| *f* | as in *foot* |
| *g* | as in *go* |
| *h* | as in *her* |
| *i* | as in *eat*, (except when preceded by c, ch, r, s, sh, z, or zh, then as in *sir*) |
| *j* | as in *jeep* |
| *k* | as in *kind* |
| *l* | as in *land* |
| *m* | as in *me* |
| *n* | as in *no* |
| *o* | as in *law* |
| *ou* | as in *owe* |
| *p* | as in *par* |
| *q* | as in *chin* |
| *r* | as in *right* |
| *s* | as in *sister* |
| *sh* | as in *shore* |
| *t* | as in *top* |
| *u* | as in *too* |
| *w* | as in *want* |
| *x* | as in *she* |
| *y* | as in *yet* |
| *z* | as in *zero* |
| *zh* | as in *jump* |

# Contents

1898–1924

THE OUTCOME OF THE BOXER REBELLION WAS A DYNASTY IN RUINS, MUCH LIKE THIS FORTRESS WHICH GUARDED THE FRONT GATE TO THE CAPITAL CITY OF BEIJING.

The scene was typical of nineteenth-century China: the sensitive young scholar wearing long robes and a pigtail, his young wife in a brocade jacket, sitting because she could not walk too far on her bound feet, and a tiny infant, their first-born. The parents both came from wealthy educated families, long established in the rich Yangzi delta area of eastern China. His father served as a high official, superintending the transport of grain and taxes up the Grand Canal, from the Yangzi river to Beijing, China's capital in the north. Her family, similarly successful, showed their affluence and culture by giving the young girl an education (in a society where female children were often considered a misfortune).

At issue was the child's name. Chinese believed that the right name should symbolize the family's and the child's fate. Fortunately, it was not too hard to decide. The father had just received the good news that he had passed the first level of the civil-service exams. The emperor's grace had been extended to him. He could look forward to a life of continuing bureaucratic advance up the ladder of success, much like his own father and elder brother. So they named the boy to commemorate the event: *the coming of grace*. The new child in the Zhou clan thus became Zhou Enlai.

But after Zhou was born on March 5, 1898, the emperor did not have much time left to bestow his grace. The events of 1900 betrayed the weakness of the dynasty. Peasant rebels working through the "Society of the Righteous and Harmonious Fists," better known in the West as the Boxers, effectively took state power into their own hands to drive out the hated foreigners. For fifty-five days in Beijing (Peking as it was known then) the foreign legations were held hostage until an international expeditionary force marched in to defeat the rebels. The dynasty could only sit by and watch from a distance. After the emperor died in 1908, imperial rule, already insubstantial, was reduced to a mere phantasm, dispelled by the 1911 Revolution.

The Zhou family declined along with the empire. Zhou Enlai's father's long-awaited imperial appointment never came. He took jobs as a sort of temporary clerk, but the solid bureaucratic posi-tion he longed for never materialized, especially after the abolition of the traditional civil-service system in 1905. His life, despite his initial hopes, became a series of part-time traveling posts which often paid little more than his own subsistence. Frequently he was unemployed, with little to do beyond sipping wine and composing poetry—the life of the traditional scholar between bureaucratic posts, without the status that might justify it.

The complex Chinese family system insulated Zhou Enlai from his father's failures, perhaps poetically, by giving him two mothers in compensation. Zhou himself never fully explained this aspect of his childhood, and the details have only come to light after his death. Apparently when Zhou was still an infant, his uncle died, leaving behind a childless widow. In situations where there was no heir, it was not uncommon for one brother to give a son to another brother, or to his widow, in order to maintain the male line of heredity. (The Chinese call this process *guoji* or "passing continuity.") Thus when Zhou Enlai was one year old he was "adopted" by his aunt. However, since his aunt was a young widow, in fact Zhou's family adopted her. Chinese accounts refer to family outings made by Zhou, his natural parents, his foster mother, and his two younger brothers. No doubt they lived in a large Chinese-style family compound which included rooms for various servants and many other members of the family. Such large provincial-gentry families were still numerous at the turn of the century, and common living quarters unquestionably took much of the emotional sting out of practices like the *guoji*.

Zhou's foster mother, well educated and vivacious, devoted her life to the young boy. Proper Chinese society frowned on widows remarrying; so young women who suddenly lost their husbands were denied any useful social function. Many committed suicide in desperation. A child provided some release from the pressures, and Zhou Enlai apparently appreciated the attention lavished on him.

Zhou received his earliest education from his foster mother. She bought the young child puzzles and games which allowed him to manipulate shapes and words even before he could hold a writing brush. Then when he was five, he began the study of calligraphy. In these crucial formative years, his foster mother guided him and imbued him with her own love of art and culture.

When Zhou was six, the family moved in with his grandfather nearby, and there Zhou received formal tutoring in the Confucian classics. The dry and heartless teaching methods then popular failed to win Zhou's affection for China's orthodox tradition. During the day he sat, like many other young gentry children with their pigtails dangling and their robes freshly cleaned, and recited the teachings of China's sages. Words of wisdom intended by scholars for rulers echoed through the centuries in schoolboy chants, often with little meaning or interest.

At night Zhou inhabited a different world. Snuggled up with his foster mother, he heard tales of ghosts and fox fairies, of martial heroes who ordered their kingdoms from horseback and not from thrones, and of revolutionary movements with liberated women who fought tyrannical emperors. This heterodox world existed only by lamplight, but still it outshone the drab Confucian world of daylight. The legends of the supernaturally mischievous *Monkey,* the *Water Margin Chronicle,* the *Romance of the Three Kingdoms,* along with stories of more modern heroes, such as the Taiping rebel Hong Xiuquan and the patriotic Commissioner Lin Zexu of the Opium War, introduced Zhou to a world only partly ruled by reason and virtue—and far more suited to China's realities.

Zhou's more heterodox education made him a skeptic at an early age. One time when his nursemaid took him along to a Buddhist temple, he noticed that the Bodhisattva's finger was broken. After staring at it a bit, he tugged on his nurse's sleeve and inquired, ''The Bodhisattva is made of clay; it's false. What use is there in praying to it?'' The scandalized country girl had no answers for his question.

Zhou's small world was destroyed by tragedy when he was only nine. His real mother fell ill and was confined to her bed just when the family fortunes were at a low ebb. His father was elsewhere and unable to send enough money home. The family's valuables had to be pawned to buy medicine, a responsibility that fell to Zhou. Scarcely as tall as the counter, he would go to the pawnshop and apothecary to get his mother's drugs. But they did

little good. Within six months she died. Then, as the Chinese say, before the first wave had subsided, the second was already rising. His foster mother contracted a similar disease. By the time he was ten, Zhou had lost his mother twice.

Decades later Zhou's voice choked with emotion whenever he mentioned his mother. On several public occasions in the 1940s, when his native province, Zhejiang, was occupied by the Japanese, he sadly recalled her and her grave choked with weeds. Which mother he meant remains a mystery, for he once told an American reporter, ''When I was still a small boy, my aunt became my true mother. Before I was ten, I never left her for a day. Then when I was ten, she and my natural mother passed away.''

Zhou's life now became far more difficult. He had been living at his maternal grandfather's house in Huaiyin. After his mother's death, the three brothers returned to their hometown of Huaian. These were hard times: famine swept the province, and even the Zhou family did not escape unscathed. Zhou had to plant a vegetable garden to feed himself and his brothers while his father went off to search for work. In the end the family could not be kept together. Zhou was sent to live with a more successful uncle in Shanghai. He later returned, but then left for good when another uncle (he had six by some accounts, only three in others) brought him to Manchuria, China's northeast, to attend school.


*EARLY SCHOOLING*

The blue bricks and red pillars of the Fengtian Dongguan Model School were still new in 1910, when the waning Qing dynasty had it built to teach the ''new learning'': history, geography, Chinese, English, physical education. Enrolled in the sixth grade for the first fall semester was twelve-year-old Zhou Enlai.

This was a new world in many ways for this slip of a boy from the south. The colder climate and harsher northern accent put him at a slight disadvantage, as did the new teaching methods, which were unlike those of his classical tutors. Yet Zhou adapted quickly and well. He developed a taste for the native grain, sorghum, which replaced his cus-

ZHOU ENLAI'S FAMILY SAVED HIM FROM THE FATE OF MANY POOR AND ORPHANED CHINESE, SUCH AS THESE FAMINE VICTIMS FORCED TO WANDER ABOUT IN SEARCH OF FOOD.

tomary rice, and soon he loved to run and play in the cold like everyone else.

This was a revolutionary time for China, and the school provided a congenial setting for Zhou's introduction to the politics of the day. He had been well prepared by his foster mother, and now for the first time he saw some of the effects of China's weakness. The Russo-Japanese War of 1904–1905 was fought on Manchurian territory. Near Shenyang, the city in Fengtian province where he now lived, Zhou witnessed the ruins of villages devastated in the war. In the school the teachers talked about these issues, and not of warring states thousands of years in the past. Zhou quite naturally became an ardent patriot under these influences—and a revolutionary. When the 1911 Revolution erupted during his second year at the school, Zhou was among the first to cut off his pigtail, the symbol of subservience to the decadent dynasty.

His fervent nationalism impressed his teachers. One in particular recalled Zhou's response to a question posed for discussion: Why should we study? Most students said they studied for their families; some said for fame or recognition. When the teacher asked Zhou, he did not know if he heard the answer right because of Zhou's soft southern accent; so he asked Zhou to repeat himself. This time the reply was unmistakable: "We should study for China to arise."

Essays surviving from these days also show Zhou to have been serious and dedicated. In a prize-winning composition he wrote, "For meeting heavy responsibilities of the future, foundations are laid in the three or four years of grade school. Fellow students, we should resolutely begin to confront our duties without regret!" However, such lofty sentiments, occasioned by a contest for essays to honor the second anniversary of the school, are not fully representative of all the interests of young Zhou.

He told an audience in 1964, "Going to Manchuria had two good points: First, it toughened my body. When I was in school, regardless of whether it was summer or winter, I wanted to go outside and strengthen my body, weak from studying. The other good point was eating sorghum. My living habits changed. My bones grew. My stomach toughened. It all made my body able to cope with years of struggle and intense work." Later, in 1966, he recommended the same regimen to young students.

By 1913 Zhou completed his studies in Shenyang. Stronger now in mind and body, he set out on his own for a school in Tianjin.

## *INDEPENDENT STUDENT*

From the small town of Huaian to the major metropolis of Shanghai to the Manchurian city of Shenyang and now to the northern Chinese port of Tianjin, in just fifteen years Zhou Enlai had traveled widely at a time when other youths had scarcely ventured beyond their village gate. The Communist leader Mao Zedong, for example, though four years older, did not enter a big city until just about this time, and had not left his small village before he was sixteen.

Of course, Zhou did not travel on his own. He had moved under the care of his uncles. Only now did he begin to act on his own, because his generally conservative uncles did not fully approve of his attendance at a reputedly "progressive" school. Zhou would have had great problems if he had had to continue to rely on their support, but his own talent and resourcefulness brought him a new protector: Zhang Boling, the principal of the Nankai Middle School of Tianjin.

Zhang Boling, a former naval officer turned educator, in some respects typified the older generation of "self-strengtheners." Horrified by China's weakness and poverty in comparison to the West, they first tried to adopt Western technology, especially arms, as the best means of self-defense. But as war after war was lost, they realized the roots of the problem reached far deeper into Chinese culture. Self-strengthening had to go beyond military self-defense, to the creation of a new culture. Principal Zhang made his contribution to this new culture through the Nankai school, which promoted student activism and self-organization, in contrast to the passive attitudes ingrained by traditional educational methods.

Zhou Enlai made a strong impression on Principal Zhang. When he entered the school, he was given advanced placement because of his high test scores. Even when placed with older students, Zhou still bettered them in literature and social

ZHOU ENLAI UPON HIS GRADUATION FROM THE NANKAI SCHOOL IN 1917.

THE AWAKENING SOCIETY AND THE FIRST ISSUE OF THEIR JOURNAL. ZHOU IS ON THE FAR RIGHT IN THE SECOND ROW. DENG YINGCHAO, HIS WIFE-TO-BE, IS THIRD FROM THE RIGHT IN THE FIRST ROW.

science, completing essays in half the time allowed—though Zhou remained consistently weak in natural science. Noticing Zhou's ability and hearing of his desire for a job, Principal Zhang hired him as a part-time secretary to work in the school office. This allowed Zhou to pay tuition, room, and board and thus be independent of his uncles' wishes.

For Zhou this must have been a very happy time. Twenty years later he would still call on Principal Zhang and recall incidents at the school. Perhaps best known was Zhou's role as the female lead in the school play *One Dollar,* in which the heroine was tempted but never succumbed to the lure of filthy lucre. Zhou's sylphlike good looks made him a natural for the part in an all-male school, but the role indicated as well the acting ability so necessary for his later career as a diplomat and political figure.

The Nankai school allowed Zhou to hone his political abilities. In keeping with Zhang Boling's general encouragement of activism, Zhou organized a small club whose purpose was revealed by its cumbersome name: "The Enjoy Work and Respect Group Life Society." Zhou also grew as a political writer. In his elementary school he wrote essays on political themes for class; at Nankai he wrote for the school newspaper. The articles reflected prevailing political opinion without much creative interpretation, but for a teenager they represented a signal accomplishment. And they should be seen as the start of Zhou's political career: the *nom de plume* he adopted for the student newspaper, Zhou Feifei or simply Feifei, he continued to use later when he was a city-wide student leader.

Zhou attended the Nankai school from 1913 to 1917. Nineteen years old when he graduated in the spring of 1917, he posed for his graduation photo looking resolutely into the future. But his actions during the next two years, two largely purposeless years spent in Japan, did not betray any firm resolution.

According to the account of a close friend at the time (who later became a hostile political opponent), Zhou arrived in Japan with very little money and even fewer plans. His friend offered to help him out, and persuaded some other Nankai alumni to contribute small amounts regularly for Zhou's support. With this aid, Zhou stayed awhile in Tokyo,

THE TIANJIN ACTIVISTS UPON THEIR RELEASE FROM JAIL. ZHOU IS SECOND FROM RIGHT IN THE FOURTH ROW.

and then moved in with his friend in Kyoto. There the usually rigorous Zhou spent his time in drinking and political discussion, without ever taking the university admission test. Life went on this way until he was suddenly called back to China in 1919.

If this account is correct, Zhou may have gone through an identity crisis in Japan. He may have been trying to decide on a career and been unsure of what steps to take. He may also have been falling into the ways of his father, who led a similar sort of life. However, Zhou did not merely discuss politics; he actively studied the concepts of Marxism then being introduced into Japan by Professor Kawakami Hajime, and he prevailed upon his friend, unsuccessfully, to introduce him to Professor Kawakami. So this may have been a period of extended political study. But whether the stay in Japan represents a psychological crisis, a momentary disorientation or the peaceful pursuit of knowledge, it ends the preparatory period in Zhou's life. Shortly after his twenty-first birthday he would return to China to help lead the May Fourth student movement and launch a public career spanning half a century.


## FROM POLITICS TO PRISON


Like Zhou's public career, China's modern political history began with the May Fourth incident and the movement which it inspired. The incident had its roots in China's political situation during World War I, when the West was preoccupied with fighting in Europe, and Japan had a free hand to intervene in China. The president of the Chinese republic at that time, Yuan Shikai, a vain and misguided ex-general who was seeking to restore the empire, with himself on the throne, was presented by Japan in January 1915 with 21 demands which, if conceded, would have placed much of China under effective Japanese control. For example, the Chinese government would have had to employ Japanese advisors, and the police in important areas would have been jointly administered by China and Japan.

President Yuan agreed to many of the lesser demands, but managed to block the most serious threats to Chinese sovereignty by leaking them to the press, provoking a public outcry from Chinese citizens and diplomatic pressure from Western countries which did not want China monopolized by Japan. Patriotic Chinese felt they had suffered a national humiliation, but expected that Japanese influence would be lessened after World War I, when Western countries would once again compete for advantages in Asia. Their hopes were strengthened when America entered the war under President Wilson's slogan of ''peace without annexations.''

But Chinese hopes were dashed when it was revealed that the Treaty of Versailles ending the war recognized the privileges which the Japanese had extorted from President Yuan (who had died in 1916). Chinese students in Beijing, already planing a demonstration, reacted to the news by going on a rampage on May 4, 1919, and beating up the cabinet minister who had signed the agreement with Japan. Merchants in Beijing shut down their shops in support of the students. Shanghai workers in Japanese-owned factories went on strike and demonstrated in the streets. Patriotic sentiment swept China like a prairie fire.

In Tianjin the movement was initially led by Ma Jun, a Moslem and close friend of Zhou Enlai at the Nankai school. Ma headed the city-wide student union which organized the public demonstration and published the *Tianjin Student,* a newpaper whose masthead proclaimed in English: ''Democracy: A government for the people, by the people, and of the people—our motto.'' It was Ma who persuaded Zhou to return from Japan with an appeal to his patriotism: ''If even our country is about to disappear, what is the use of studying?''

Upon receipt of Ma's message, Zhou packed his bags, borrowed some money, and left Japan within days. Back in Tianjin, he was heartily welcomed by his former schoolmates and quickly elected editor-in-chief of the newspaper. The 21-year-old journalist rapidly revised the paper's format from the literary to the vernacular style and expanded the readership. Originally a biweekly, the paper expanded into a daily with a circulation of 20,000. Zhou's editorials and articles, appearing under his old by-line ''Feifei,'' influenced broad segments of the society.

Formally Zhou was once again a student. He registered at Nankai University, an offshoot of his former school, also run by Principal Zhang, but apparently did so only to get a clerical job to support himself. By most accounts his time was taken up totally by the newspaper. He showed up early each morning with an editorial composed over a breakfast of bean-curd soup which he ate at a small stand on the way. The rest of the day would be given to the details of publishing, and Zhou had final responsibility until the paper went out in the late afternoon or evening. This schedule left no time for classes.

The movement peaked during the summer months. By the fall of 1919, Zhou was able to devote more time to long-term organizing. Like other May Fourth activists throughout the country, he saw the need for planned action rather than spontaneous reaction. To respond to this need, he was instrumental in establishing the "Awakening Society," composed of about twenty top student leaders. Unlike previous organizations, the Awakening Society included women, who previously had only an ancillary role, as the Association of Patriotic Women Comrades. This new society stood to the left of the main movement and espoused the general philosophy of the need to "awaken" the people. Formally founded September 17, 1919, it produced the first issue of its journal *Awakening* on January 20, 1920. A week later, in a separate incident, Zhou Enlai was arrested.

Trouble with the police had begun much earlier in the fall. As the movement subsided, the police cracked down on student activities. In one raid on the newspaper, Zhou barely escaped arrest. Police increased the pressure by completely shutting down the paper in November. But anti-Japanese protests continued, and when more than twenty student demonstrators were arrested in January, Zhou led a large contingent to the provincial governor's offices to demand their release.

A high wall surrounded the governor's offices, and by the time the protest march reached it, the main gate had been barred. The students stood outside shouting for awhile, but to no avail. Suddenly someone discovered that a lower section of the gate could be opened to give a foot or so of space. Injudiciously, Zhou and three others crawled under, only to be arrested the instant they stood up. The protest outside fizzled, while Zhou and his three comrades were marched off to join the students they had come to free.

Since the protests were in large part directed against the police for failing to support the students' patriotic activities, the police chief, Yang Yide, felt it best not to give the students a public forum and tried to hold them incommunicado. For several months, they were not allowed to talk to one another nor were they taken to court. Chief Yang's plans were foiled, however, when Zhou Enlai discovered that the students could meet in the toilet area before roll call in the morning. Here furtive plots were hatched by a committee and the word spread by messages written on toilet paper and dropped into cells. Yang soon had a hunger strike on his hands and was forced to allow them to stand trial.

Once the case was brought to court, the students were able to win privileges in jail. They were allowed to meet together and conduct study sessions. Zhou later published a diary of this period, and the entries show him to have been one of the intellectual leaders of the group. A typical entry reads:

"May 31. Today classes reported some slight changes. Apart from studying English, mathematics, history, and geography, everybody also studied Japanese, psychology, and economics. The study of economics was led by Ma Qianli; Japanese and psychology were led by Zhou Enlai. In the afternoon Sha Zhupei was examined in court. In the evening everyone gathered for a lecture given by Zhou Enlai on Marxism and historical materialism."

Public pressure brought by the members of the Awakening Society and a number of prominent citizens forced the students' release after six months in prison. On July 17, 1920, Zhou and the others were freed; they posed for a group photo to commemorate their victory.

Zhou stayed in Tianjin long enough to celebrate his freedom, but soon he was preparing to go abroad again, this time to France.


## COMMUNIST ORGANIZER IN EUROPE

Even before his departure for Europe, Zhou was engaged in Communist organizing. In late 1919 he apparently made several trips to Beijing, where the

ZHOU IN TAINJIN, JUST BEFORE HIS DEPARTURE
FOR EUROPE.

IN EARLY 1921 ZHOU VISITED LONDON, WHERE THIS PICTURE WAS
TAKEN.

young chief librarian of Beijing University, Li Dazhao, had formed a society for the study of socialism. The society, which included among it members such leading student activists as Mao Zedong from the southern Chinese province of Hunan, went beyond theory and made contact with representatives of the Comintern (the Third or Communist International then being organized by Lenin). Eventually, Communist groups would be formed in China, and Zhou was very much involved in the early planning stages. He took a group to meet with the Comintern representative, Sergei Polevoy, in Tianjin.

But Communist organizing faced two major problems. The authorities all over the country were throwing radicals into jail—Zhou was not alone in this experience—and the ideas of socialism and communism were relatively new and poorly understood, even by many left-wing theorists. Both to escape further arrests and to conduct their studies, a number of student radicals, including Zhou, went abroad.

Zhou chose France, which had a unique appeal for Chinese students. Since 1903 Chinese educators, influenced by the ideals of the French Revolution, had been sending Chinese students to France in a program of combined work and study. The French government supported this program, no doubt hoping to extend its political influence in China. During the labor shortage caused by World War I, the program expanded. In 1920 an estimated 1,600 Chinese were working and studying in France. In addition, a much larger number of coolie laborers, possibly as many as 200,000, were spread throughout France and its colonies, engaged in postwar reconstruction. Chinese students could feel at home in this large overseas community.

The radical Chinese students in Paris welcomed Zhou. After his arrival in November 1920, he sent a friend a postcard—oddly enough the picture on the front was of Zhou and not of Paris—and wrote. "Paris beautiful! Many friends, many sights. Would you like to come?"

In Paris Zhou spent most of his time at work and on politics. Schooling was limited to a brief period at the College de Chateau Thierry to learn some usable French. Because of the language problem, he may have considered going to school in England, here his fluent English would have been an

ZHOU IN PARIS, 1923.

THE PARISIAN BRANCH OF THE CHINESE COMMUNIST PARTY. ZHOU IS FRONT ROW CENTER.

THE PARISIAN BRANCH OF THE CHINESE SOCIALIST YOUTH CORPS. ZHOU IS SIXTH FROM THE RIGHT IN THE FRONT ROW. DENG XIAOPING, THEN ZHOU'S ASSISTANT, IS ON THE RIGHT IN THE FOURTH ROW.

asset, but after a brief visit there he returned to France, where he elected to do informal study using English-language materials. Thus it was in France that the Chinese Zhou Enlai studied the German Karl Marx in English translation.

Zhou, however, devoted himself more to practical affairs than to cloistered study. Five and a half days a week he worked as a mechanic in the Renault automobile factory in the Parisian suburb of Billancourt. Lodged in a simple room nearby, he spent his evenings writing poetry and letters home. The writings reveal his increasing radicalization. The poems refer to "Communist flowers blossoming" and "the red flag flying over the whole world." To the Awakening Society back in Tianjin, he wrote, "To sum up, on ideological matters, we nearly all agree. If I were to summarize it all in a few words, they would be, 'We should believe in the theory of communism and in the two great principles of class revolution and the dictatorship of the proletariat, and in the effective methods appropriate to the circumstances.' "

On the weekends he shed his worker's overalls and, dressed in a respectable bourgeois suit, went downtown to the cafes where Chinese students gathered to discuss the revolution at home and abroad. Zhou quickly emerged as a leader among these radical youth, even though some of them had been in Paris quite a bit longer. Thus Zhou organized the largest demonstration of Chinese students held in France; this was in Lyons in September 1921.

At Lyons a new university was built with French and Chinese monies to cope with the large Chinese student population. Protests arose when the school announced that it would only accept newly arrived students. Radicals in Paris suspected a political motivation; the newer students could be closely screened and leftists weeded out. They decided to organize a demonstration.

Plans were made in Paris, where most of the students were. Zhou came every night to meetings right from work and still in his overalls. They decided to gather in Lyons and march on the school. Zhou was to stay in Paris to handle the final details and then join the demonstrators already gathering in Lyons. On September 20, dressed in his work clothes and carrying a briefcase packed with papers and pamphlets, Zhou left Paris and headed southeast for Lyons.

On September 21, a Wednesday, hundreds of Chinese students had arrived in Lyons. The panicked police called the Chinese legation, which dismissed the students as "radical troublemakers." Freed from the threat of an international incident, the police moved in and rounded up the demonstrators. They were held in army barracks and eventually more than a hundred were deported.

Zhou, out of jail for only a little more than a year, escaped arrest and made it back to Paris. Throughout the remainder of the year, he kept a low profile to avoid the attention of French and Chinese authorities. This set the pattern for the next two years, during which he gave up his job and became somewhat of a man of mystery, shuttling back and forth between Paris and Berlin with no apparent source of income or fixed occupation. In fact, Zhou had become a professional revolutionary.

Details on this period are few. Fellow Chinese describe visiting him at a luxurious flat on Wilhelmstrasse in Berlin and finding him comfortably accoutred and willing to spend the afternoon chatting. Quite a change from his days in the Renault factory!

But luxury served only as a front to disguise his subversive activities as a Communist organizer. The Chinese Communist party had been established in Shanghai in July 1921, and a European branch followed in six months. While he was organizing the Lyons demonstration, Zhou must have also been preparing for the formation of a party group. After some of the other organizers were deported because of the demonstration or had left to study in the Soviet Union, Zhou assumed key responsibilities in the organization. From the start he headed the larger youth group, the Socialist Youth Corps, and his central role in the party is suggested by his prominent position in the 1924 photograph of the Parisian party group.

His party work broke down into three categories: recruitment, writing, and liaison work. His most famous recruit was Zhu De, the former revolutionary turned warlord, whose early patriotism brought him into the 1911 revolution and set him on a military career that, like so many others at the time, ended in corruption and opium addiction. Zhu De came to Europe to shake his habit and, if

ZHOU IN BERLIN.

possible, rejoin the revolution, for the Communists in Shanghai had rejected him. So one day he showed up at the Wilhelmstrasse apartment and appealed to the slender young intellectual, telling him that the past was like ashes under his feet—completely destroyed and forgotten. Zhou Enlai listened quietly to the appeal, then replied he would see what he could do. Through Zhou Enlai's intercession, Zhu De was admitted to the party and went on to become the most famous general in the Red Army. (Deng Xiaoping, the most powerful man in China today, was also one of Zhou's Parisian recruits.)

Writing for the party was done in the small journal *Youth*, where Zhou used his Awakening Society pseudonym Wu Hao. His articles set out the party position on a broad range of topics; although some of his articles were criticized for a lack of creativity, everyone agreed that Zhou's articles were the clearest and most succinct presentations yet done. This ease of expression might have been expected from someone who had been working on newspapers off and on for ten years, ever since his days at the Nankai school. And even while he wrote for the party, he continued to send articles on European affairs to Tianjin newspapers as a source of extra income.

Liaison work also benefited from Zhou's fluency of expression. A peacemaker since childhood, Zhou was often the only person who could hold together the fractious Chinese students. He could work behind the scenes, dealing with small groups to plan demonstrations, and on the public platform, where he could appeal to the common interests of the audience. But even Zhou's talents weren't enough to hold together a left wing composed of communists, nationalists, and anarchists. After the formal merger of the Communists and Nationalists in the Nationalist party headed by Dr. Sun Yatsen, the republican revolutionary and first president, the anarchists took to starting fights and even carrying guns at meetings. At first, in late 1923, Zhou stepped in to stop fights, but by the spring of 1924 he gave up on his peacemaking attempts. In an uncommon burst of passion at a Nationalist party meeting, he blasted the anarchists with these words:

"They talk and talk about petitions and strikes, but when there is a demonstration, who marches at the head of the column to face the guns and clubs of the police, get beat up, jailed, and even butchered? It is we, the Nationalist party cadres, not they! They talk about assassination and terrorism, but it is the Nationalist party comrades' blood that is shed, not theirs."

Soon afterward, in August 1924, Zhou was recalled to China to work full-time on the nationalist revolution. His work there would make him world-famous—as a literary character!

1924–1927

SUN YATSEN AND HIS WIFE, SONG QINGLING.

The guard outside the hotel stood impassively as the stream of Chinese, with the occasional foreigner mixed in, passed by. Suddenly out of the corner of his eye he noticed a figure dressed in khaki with a Sam Browne belt accenting his uniform. The man was young; the smoothness of his face might suggest a beginning cadet to the unwary. But the guard recognized the bearing of intelligence and command. He snapped a stiff salute as Zhou Enlai entered the hotel.

Within months of his return from Europe, Zhou was widely known and respected as a successful soldier. The former actor, editor, auto worker, and organizer slipped into his new career as easily as another might slip on a pair of gloves, but the change was not as dramatic as one very far from the scene might suspect. The explanation lay in the unique relationship between the military and Sun Yatsen.

A Christian convert trained in medicine in Hong Kong, Sun Yatsen belonged to that generation of revolutionaries who dreamed of a strong and prosperous China and schemed for the downfall of the Manchus. Their schemes worked, for the dynasty did fall, but their dreams remained unfulfilled as political power passed into the hands of the military, whose leaders were derogatorily called "warlords." As the warlords fought each other for power and in the process divided China into countless satrapies, Sun hatched plans for a new revolution, the first step of which would be the military reunification of the country and the removal of the warlords.

But Sun's plans faced the problem of all strategies which propose to fight fire with fire: he was regularly burnt by the same militarism he proposed to eliminate. Throughout the 1920s a number of his military collaborators rebelled against his authority. One erstwhile colleague, Chen Jiongming, led rebellions in June 1922, May 1923, November 1924, and January 1925. Sun had to overcome not just miltary leaders, but an entire military system.

His answer to the problem was the introduction of the Soviet political-commissar system, recently generated by the civil war in Russia. In order to construct a reliable army in the shortest time possible, the Russian Communists subordinated prerevolutionary officers to Communist party representatives known as political commissars. Sun in similar fashion placed politically reliable young officers in charge of less dependable but more experienced commanders.

Zhou Enlai was one of the young party members serving as a political commissar in Sun's army. Officially he held the position of deputy director of the political department of the Nationalist party's military academy. In fact the director, a long-time Nationalist, left most of the work and responsibility to the 26-year-old Communist. The trust proved justified in early 1925, when Zhou kept to the front lines and rallied the troops during the final showdown with Chen Jiongming. Zhou's part in the victory over Chen made him widely known and respected in military circles.

But Zhou remained concerned primarily with politics, because ultimately it was politics that would shape the fate of the revolution. As in Europe, the Chinese revolutionaries back home shared common goals, but broke down into hostile factions over the methods to achieve those goals. Until his sudden death from cancer at age 58 in March 1925, Sun Yatsen acted as a unifying force. With him gone, factionalism started to pull the revolution apart. Zhou worked to keep it together.

The issue creating the most confusion was Communist membership in the Nationalist party. In early 1925, fewer than one thousand Communist party members had joined the Nationalist party, whose membership was at least four times as great and whose political influence was substantial. Yet the Communists joined as individuals while keeping their previous membership in the Communist party. So the question arose: Was their first loyalty to the Nationalist party or to the Communist party? For example, was Zhou Enlai acting as a political director for the Nationalists or as military director (a position he concurrently held) for the Communists?

In many situations dual loyalties would have produced unbearable strains, but the Nationalist party was already riven with factionalism hard for the outsider to comprehend. Ancient regional hostilities influenced friendships and associations. Political and ideological differences played a part. In short, the complex crazy quilt of Chinese social

REVOLUTIONARY TROOPS UNDER SUN.

RIGHT: ZHOU ENLAI AS A POLITICAL COMMISSAR.

SUN YATSEN HAD CLOSE TIES TO THE RUSSIAN COMMUNISTS IN HIS FINAL YEARS. HERE SUN (CENTER, IN WHITE HAT) ATTENDS MEETING TO COMMEMORATE THE RUSSIAN LEADER LENIN, WHO DIED A YEAR BEFORE SUN.

relations filtered into the Chinese Nationalist party. The Communist-Nationalist split was only one division among many others.

Before his death Sun Yatsen certainly did not see any great chasm between Communism and his own Nationalist ideas, which he called the Three Principles of the People (or nationalism, democracy, and people's livelihood). As he wrote in what has been called the Nationalist party's "Bible":

"We cannot say, then, that the theory of communism is different from our principle of the people's livelihood. Our Three Principles of the People mean government 'of the people, by the people, and for the people.'... If this is true, the people will have not only a communistic share in state production, but a share in everything."

But the right wing of the Nationalist party, which had opposed Sun's admission of the Communists and his friendship with the Soviet Union from the very beginning, chose to emphasize passages where Sun wrote "today we can take Marx's ideas as a guide, but we cannot make use of his methods," and to interpret them as wholesale rejections of Communism.

The right wing opposed Communism partly for generational reasons. Most of them were older than the Communists who had come of age during the May Fourth Movement, when the West looked particularly bad and the Russian Revolution exerted powerful attraction. For the older generation, Russia remained just another country not to be trusted, and May Fourth was schoolboy rowdyism. They saw no reason for radical youth coming in and taking over, especially if the youth were merely stalking horses for the Soviet Union. The right, not surprisingly, conveniently ignored the fact that it was Sun Yatsen who introduced the Communists and Russian advisors into the party to overcome preexisting problems.

Throughout 1925, Zhou Enlai resolutely fought these factional tendencies. In a Nationalist party forum, he reiterated Sun Yatsen's goals: "First, unite Guangdong; second, unite China; third, smash imperialism." In other words, first secure their southern provincial base, from there reunite the country, then deal with foreign intervention. The key, the first step, had to be unity.

Unity did not come easily. In a right-wing ploy against the Communists, a former aide of Zhou's was lured into a compromising situation in which the gunboat under his command appeared to be placed for a *coup d'etat* against the Nationalist army commander Chiang Kaishek. Chiang, a shrewd politician who believed in an updated Confucianism with a military flavor, used the purported coup attempt to reduce the power of the Communists— and of the right—and thereby strengthened his own position.

Zhou lost his political posts in the aftermath of the coup, but his talents could not be wasted. Once it became clear that Chiang was not purging the Communists and was keeping his distance from the right wing, Zhou resumed much of his work as political commissar. He gave the troops political instruction, taught classes at the peasant leadership training academy (run by Mao Zedong, also then a Communist in the Nationalist party), and helped assign officers to the troops preparing for the northern expedition to reunify China. However, his fame would come not as a political commissar, but as an insurrectionist.

### THE FAITHFUL HUSBAND

Zhou Enlai was always too much the gentleman and the Communist to reveal much of his personal life. He talked of China and the revolution, and the personal needs and cares of others, but not of himself. As a result, his love for and marriage to Deng Yingchao assumes the appearance of impersonal comradeship.

Zhou met Deng on his return from Japan in 1919. Deng, a short, round-faced girl, did not initially attract Zhou. He had an old girl friend whom he saw until her family sent her abroad a few weeks after Zhou's return. However, Deng led the Association of Patriotic Women Comrades, and her widowed mother often let her use their house for political meetings. Soon proximity and the charm of this lively high-school girl worked their magic on Zhou. While he was in France he wrote her regularly, though how much was personal and how much purely political we do not know.

When Zhou returned to China in 1924, he lived in the southern city of Guangzhou, the capital of Guangdong province and the center of revolutionary activities. Deng still lived in Tianjin, far to the

DENG YINGCHAO AND ZHOU ENLAI IN YANAN, 1936.

north. She had joined the Communist party on her own and then the Nationalist party. Like Zhou she was ordered to Guangzhou, where she headed the women's department of the Nationalist party. Reunited in 1925, they decided to marry.

Theirs was a modern marriage of equals. Despite all the talk of "modern" youth and sexual revolution, China still had arranged marriages and concubinage, which affected the sexual ethos of the times. Divorces were frequent, and liaisons came easy. But Zhou and Deng represented the ideal of two dedicated activists sharing their lives in a common cause. Zhou even did some of the cooking! Nonetheless, they were people of their time and social rank. Often the housework was done by servants or aides, and both were usually too busy to devote much time to domestic affairs. Childless (apparently not by choice), they devoted themselves to the revolution, and for fifty years made a formidable team in politics and diplomacy.

## THE INSURRECTIONIST

In *Man's Fate* by Andre Malraux, the famous French art critic and novelist, the protagonist Kyo Gisors, half-French and half-Japanese, walks the streets of Shanghai the night before a planned insurrection:

"Since he had started to prepare the insurrection more than a month ago, working from committee to committee, he had ceased to see the streets: he no longer walked in the mud but on a map. The scratching of millions of small daily lives disappeared, crushed by another life. The concessions, the rich quarters, with their rain-washed gratings at the ends of the streets, existed now only as menaces, barriers, long prison walls without windows; these atrocious quarters, on the contrary—the ones in which the shock troops (of the revolution) were the most numerous—were alive with the quivering of a multitude lying in wait.... After the failure of the February uprising, the Central Committee of the Chinese Communist party had entrusted Kyo with the coordination of the insurrectional forces."

Coordination, in fact, was entrusted to someone who had studied in France and Japan, but who was fully Chinese, Zhou Enlai. Yet, despite his youthful days in Shanghai, the real Zhou must have

DENG YINGCHAO AND ZHOU ENLAI IN NANJING, 1946.

OPPOSITE: THE STREETS OF SHANGHAI: THE BUND.

THE STREETS OF SHANGHAI: FUZHOU ROAD.

shared the fictional Kyo's concerns. It would be no easy task to direct the efforts of Shanghai's 800,000 revolutionary workers.

Shanghai's workers had been a political force since the May Fourth Movement of 1919. In 1925 they exploded again and shut the city down after a Japanese factory guard killed a Communist labor organizer and British-supervised police fired on a protest demonstration. This 1925 general strike spread to Guangzhou, and turned the national political climate toward revolution. By the end of the year, the Shanghai strike was suppressed, but the Guangzhou events had resulted in the northern expedition, which was approaching Shanghai in the spring of 1927. Control of the city with all its foreign trade revenues was a major revolutionary goal.

The workers themselves had already attempted to seize the city twice. In October 1926, they planned to rise up after the defection of a local warlord's subordinate. The subordinate defected with his troops, but the insurrection never materialized. A rocket, intended to signal a gunboat to begin firing, was not seen by the gunboat. Without hearing the ship's guns, the insurrectionists continued to wait for a signal to start. As a result, there were only a few skirmishes with the police by isolated, impatient groups. The warlord's subordinate and his troops were defeated while waiting for the insurrectionists to come to their aide.

In February 1927, a more serious attempt ran into similar problems. The revolutionary trade union leadership decided to call a general strike, but left it to the Communist party to carry out the insurrection. The Communists, caught by surprise, needed time to coordinate their actions. The Shanghai warlord, Sun Chuanfang, benefited from the delay. He ordered several of the strike's leaders executed, and threatened every striker with death. The general strike of 200,000 went into decline. At this point the Communists made their move. Revolutionary gunboats seized the arsenal, and the police in key districts came under attack. It was too late. In the two main working-class districts, the insurrection failed. In Zhabei, to the north, once again they did not hear the gunboat. In Pudong, to the east, the insurgents were outnumbered and defeated by the police. Plagued with other problems, including reduced morale because of the decline of the general strike, the Communist command center called off any further actions.

Zhou Enlai arrived in Shanghai shortly afterward. He had to overcome the poor planning that had so far sabotaged the insurrectionary attempts. He knew he did not have much time. Sun Chuanfang had made some bold moves, but had done little more because demoralization was spreading among his troops. If the political climate shifted against the revolutionaries, Sun would surely unleash a white terror against the workers.

One of Zhou's first steps was to isolate Sun. Politically much had been done already, but economically and militarily Sun continued to receive fresh supply lines. When Sun's troops tried to order the railwaymen back at gunpoint, the workers sabotaged the tracks and derailed the trains.

Next Zhou built up his own forces. A better command structure was organized, and each commander, like the fictional Kyo Gisors, had to study his area in great detail so that any problems could be anticipated.

Finally, in a political touch typical of Zhou, a delegate assembly, representing all parts of the city, elected an executive committee to assume political authority after the insurrection. No one was excluded from the 26-member committee, which included only fifteen Communists. Zhou thus made sure that the insurrection could not be interpreted as a factional power grab.

By March 21, the 6,000 organized insurrectionists with their 150 guns were ready to face 2,000 fully armed police and 3,000 warlord troops, equipped with an armored train and white Russian advisors.

The noon whistle blew. Suddenly the city went dead. Trolley cars stopped. Electricity and water were shut off. An unnatural quiet reigned as the insurgent workers converged on the local police stations. At 1:00 precisely, attacks began, and the outnumbered police surrendered without a fight. In less than an hour, the insurgents increased their weapon supply tenfold. The only serious fighting broke out in Zhabei, where warlord troops and their Russian advisors tried to hold the train station and rail lines. By 4:00 P.M. the next day, they too, complete with the armored train, were defeated. Shanghai belonged to the revolution.

Zhou, who personally led the attack on the Post

Office, must have been dumbfounded by the next turn of events. Within hours after vanquishing the warlord troops, the workers sent out delegates bearing cookies and hot towels to welcome the National Revolutionary Army troops who had finally reached the edge of the city. Their general, Bai Chongxi, an old-fashioned militarist enlisted in the revolutionary cause, greeted them coldly. He did not approve of workers upstaging his soldiers, and demanded that the workers hand over their arms and return to work. In succeeding days he more ominously repeated his demand, as he restored much of the old power structure. The police force simply received a new chief, a member of the Nationalist party's right wing.

Zhou and other Communist party leaders hotly debated the significance of these moves. Zhou and other younger party members argued that the workers must be prepared to defend themselves if necessary. Chen Duxiu, the party general secretary and a former professor, advised continued cooperation, not thinking that the matter was immediately serious.

Zhou, Chen, and the other Communists did not know that Chiang Kaishek, who did not seem to be involved, was planning his own *coup d'etat.* Weeks earlier, wealthy Shanghai businessmen who bankrolled the Nationalist party's right wing had visited him during a lull in the fighting and promised to finance his political future if he would come over to their side. Chiang, the ''Red General'' who publicly denounced imperialism and proclaimed Moscow the center of the world revolution, accepted their offer. But he did not let his change of heart be known.

In Shanghai itself Yu Xiaqing, the head of the Chinese Chamber of Commerce, conspired with Du Yuesheng, Shanghai's premier gangster and opium dealer, and Stirling Fessenden, the American ''mayor'' of the foreign community. Together they possessed the three crucial ingredients for a coup: money, men, and surprise. Yu provided funds for Du's gangster brigades. Fessenden supplied the unprecedented permission for armed Chinese to pass through the foreign concession area, ordinarily a virtual foreign country beyond Chinese control, and spring a surprise attack on union headquarters in Zhabei, command center for the workers' revolt.

Early on the morning of April 12, 1927, armed thugs disguised as workers assaulted union headquarters. The few workers inside were confused. Zhou Enlai, who had been there during the night on other matters, instantly realized a coup was being attempted and commanded the workers to fight back. But the surprise caught them off guard and too unprepared. Before the day was out, they surrendered, and Zhou was arrested.

Zhou's life was in serious danger. Du Yuesheng's men had murdered the head of the trade unions in cold blood as the first move in the coup. Other leaders were similarly killed outright. Zhou, working under his pseudonym of Wu Hao, was not recognized as the military commander of the insurrection, and was handed over to Bai Chongxi's troops for interrogation. According to one story, Bai walked in during Zhou's questioning and was impressed by his courage, but, luckily for Zhou, did not realize his identity. A young aide with radical sympathies did, but kept quiet. That night the aide came to free Zhou and slip him past the guards. He quickly fled the city.

Behind him he left a labor movement in defeat. More than 117,000 workers struck to protest Chiang's coup, but their demonstrations bore the brunt of suppression by ex-warlord troops now under Chiang's command. Even when women and children stood in the front, the soldiers mercilessly fired directly into the crowd. With leaders dead or in hiding and the bodies of militants lying in the street, the strike collapsed, and Shanghai was lost.

Zhou escaped up the Yangzi river to Wuhan, where the civilian Nationalist government opposed Chiang's unilateral move and still cooperated with the Communists. Wuhan at this time was in chaos. To the normal confusion of a revolutionary process, there was now added all the problems of Chiang's betrayal. What did it mean for the Communist party? For that matter, what did it do to the Nationalist party, whose successes so far had depended on Soviet aid and Communist cooperation.

In an elementary school, some eighty delegates to a Communist party congress met to discuss these questions. In the darkness of the times, their deliberation generated heat rather than light. They knew they had to oppose Chiang Kaishek, but could not decide what that implied. Chen Duxiu, the older and calmer party general secretary, backed by the

SHANGHAI'S SUZHOU CREEK.

THE STREETS OF SHANGHAI: NANJING ROAD.

SHANGHAI'S HUANGPU RIVER.

IN THE MID-1920s, CHINA'S CITIES EXPLODED WITH NATIONALIST SENTIMENT. HERE STUDENTS IN BEIJING DEMONSTRATE IN FAVOR OF BOYCOTTING ENGLISH AND JAPANESE GOODS.

RIGHT: THIS STUDENT DID HIS UTMOST TO GET THE MESSAGE ACROSS. THE CHARACTERS ON HIS BACK SAY THAT EVERYONE HAS THE RESPONSIBILITY TO BOYCOTT ENGLISH AND JAPANESE GOODS AND TO OVERSEE THE GOVERNMENT'S NEGOTIATIONS. AFTER 1919 THE STUDENTS FELT THE REGULAR GOVERNMENT COULD NOT BE TRUSTED, AND THIS STUDENT, WITH THE NATIONALIST PARTY FLAG STUCK IN HIS ARMBAND, CLEARLY EXPRESSED HIS PREFERENCE FOR AN ALTERNATIVE.

IN SHANGHAI THE WORKERS DID NOT MERELY PROTEST. THEY ARMED THEMSELVES FOR REVOLUTION.

WARLORD TROOPS ALSO ARMED THEMSELVES. THE "GRENADE CORPS" SEEN HERE WAS SUPPOSED TO MAKE A LAST-DITCH DEFENSE OF THE CITY. THEY DID BETTER WHEN POSING FOR WESTERN NEWSMEN.

FOR SEVERAL WEEKS IN THE SPRING OF 1927, SHANGHAI'S WORKERS RULED THE CITY. HERE IS A PUBLIC MEETING OF THE SHANGHAI GENERAL UNION, THE CITY-WIDE FEDERATION OF LABOR UNIONS.

OPPOSITE: IN EARLY APRIL 1927, TROOPS UNDER THE COMMAND OF CHIANG KAISHEK MOVED INTO SHANGHAI TO MAINTAIN "ORDER."

CASUALTIES BEGAN TO MOUNT AS TROOPS ATTEMPTED TO DISARM THE WORKERS.

ON APRIL 12, 1927, GANGSTER FORCES LAUNCHED A FULL-SCALE ATTACK ON THE WORKERS' HEADQUARTERS. HERE A WORKER IS LED OFF BY A GANGSTER (IN WHITE TURBAN) AND ONE OF CHIANG'S SOLDIERS.

IN GUANGZHOU IN THE SOUTH, THE REVOLUTIONARY WORKERS WERE CUT DOWN IN THE STREETS, AND THE BODIES LEFT THERE UNTIL THEY BEGAN TO STINK.

A MODERN ARTIST'S CONCEPTION OF THE NANCHANG UPRISING.   ZHOU (WITHOUT HAT) ADDRESSES THE TROOPS.

Soviet advisor Borodin (and therefore the Comintern), counseled caution and keeping the alliance with the Nationalist party as long as possible. Qu Qiubai, a more radical young Communist writer and journalist, wanted to shed the Nationalist ties and deepen the revolution. The congress compromised. Zhou Enlai was elected to the political bureau, the highest level of the party, and continued as head of military affairs. His assignment was to carry out the new policies.

But the Communists did not control events. One after the other, the Nationalist generals joined Chiang Kaishek. By July the Wuhan government was isolated and without significant military support. Wang Jingwei, the vacillating civilian head of state, bowed to the political momentum and went over to Chiang. There could be no compromising now; the Communists were on their own.

## FOUNDER OF THE RED ARMY

The counterrevolution purged the Communists from the top. The Communists responded by rising up from below. Within weeks of their expulsion from Wuhan in central China, Zhou Enlai and others led their own rebellion in Nanchang, a city 130 miles to the southeast. Ironically, they claimed to be acting in the name of the Nationalist party.

The mechanics of the revolt were comparatively simple. Although the highest echelons of the National Revolutionary Army generally opposed the Communists, many younger officers supported them. The garrison commander of Nanchang not only supported them but secretly was one. Zhu De, after being recruited by Zhou in Berlin, had returned to China with his party membership kept secret. Since he had a warlord background, he rose easily in the Nationalist officer hierarchy, which Chiang Kaishek carefully shielded from Communist influence. Zhou relied on Zhu De and his troops to form the core of the uprising.

Zhou also persuaded some non-Communist commanders to join the rebellion. He Long, a warlord from a military family famous for its bravery, and Ye Ting, a division commander with strong Nationalist party credentials, agreed to rally their troops to the banner of the "Central Revolutionary Committee," ostensibly the left wing of the Nationalist party, but almost entirely Communist in composition.

On August 1, 1927, the Nanchang garrison declared its independence from Chiang Kaishek, and announced the formation of the new committee to continue the revolution. The next day Zhou Enlai delivered a public address, spelling out the principles of the new regime. But superior forces were already marching on the city. Faced with the threat of encirclement and defeat, Zhou ordered a retreat on August 4.

The troops headed south, retracing the victorious advance of the previous year, when the peasant revolution had forced out warlord and landlord alike. Now they encountered widespread devastation in the wake of the counterrevolution. Landlords had returned with insatiable hatred in their hearts. Peasant leaders were beaten, tortured, mutilated, burned alive. Agricultural production was so disrupted that many escaped the landlords only to face starvation. Surrounded by such desolation, the Communist troops made their long and bitter trek south.

By the time they reached China's southern coast, Zhou had fallen ill, and the main body of troops had been decimated. Beset with malaria, Zhou could barely walk. He had to be helped onto a ship, which brought him to the relatively safe haven of Hong Kong, where he was hospitalized. The troops similarly suffered from disease, and, because they had lost their former base of support among the peasants, also from defeat and desertions. Nevertheless, from these ragtag remnants, eventually the Red Army would emerge and would trace its origins back to the Nanchang Uprising of August 1, 1927. As a commander of the uprising, Zhou Enlai is therefore credited as a founder of the Red Army. However, Zhou's future would lie with politics, not the military.

1927–1935

In 1928 the Zhou family compound in Shanghai had two new members, Seventh Brother Xiangyu and his wife Yingchao. The matriarch of the household had raised him for nearly five years while he was still young and welcomed him back. Thirteenth Brother Enzhu, twenty years old and already a father, was also happy about his older cousin's return.

For several years Xiangyu and Yingchao brightened the lives of the family. Xiangyu particularly delighted his aunt, the matriarch, by catering to her tastes. He took her and rest of the family to the movies because she was especially fond of them and he conducted all the religious ceremonies because, as his aunt once gushed, "Xiangyu knows all the rules and does everything *just right*." Thirteenth Brother Enzhu received his share of attention. Xiangyu interceded with his aunt when she censured young Enzhu's interest in Beijing opera, and Xiangyu would frequently go out with Enzhu. Nor was Enzhu's wife, Shunyi, forgotten. A member of the family by an arranged marriage, she ordinarily would have been ignored, but Yingchao watched over her and her babies like an elder sister. When the babies were sick, Xiangyu, their uncle, often took greater interest than Enzhu, their father. Altogether, a most idyllic scene, but it was only half of the double lives of Zhou Enlai and Deng Yingchao.

After Chiang's coup, Zhou Enlai was a wanted man with a price on his head. He had tried to escape to a safe area, but soon there were none, as the white terror took its toll. Even the former revolutionary capital of Guangzhou was not safe. After an insurrection failed there in December, 4,000 workers were mercilessly slaughtered. Hope for survival was greatest in the cosmopolitan environs of Shanghai, where multiple police jurisdictions, the high volume of trade and travelers, and the Zhou family compound offered some protection from the prying eyes of the secret police. For four years, from 1927 to 1931, the party's central committee would operate underground in Shanghai, where each member cultivated an innocent-appearing separate existence. At home Zhou Enlai was Xiangyu, his aunt's old name for him, while in the party he adopted a new *nom de guerre*, Shao Shan. The police, meanwhile, continued to search for Zhou Enlai.

Within the party responsibility for counterespionage fell to Zhou. From his time directing the Shanghai insurrection, he knew a tobacco worker and secret-society member who had staunchly fought for the revolution. Somewhat of a dandy, this Shanghai-lander, Gu Shunzhang, was appointed to head the party's own secret service. Gu quickly went about using his connections to the Green Gang, the very same secret society from which Du Yuesheng recruited his gangsters, to infiltrate the secret services of the Nationalist party and the various police forces, both Chinese and foreign. By early 1928 the party had advance notice of impending raids and was able to prevent major arrests. Gu, an accomplished magician as well, then went on the road as a performer and extended the counterspy system to other cities. With self-defense taken care of, the next question was a new offensive strategy.

The strategy was formulated in Moscow. In the late spring of 1928, about thirty delegates from all over China headed north for the Trans-Siberian Railroad and thence to a secluded suburban manor, where they spent weeks rehashing the events of the previous year. Contrasts there could not have been greater. The aristocratic splendor of the house's structure clashed with the spartan cots and tables gathered for the delegates' use. The world-historic judgments and revolutionary experience of the participants belied their relative youth. Zhou Enlai, after a decade in politics, was only thirty years old. Nikolai Bukharin, the short, balding "Old Bolshevik" overseeing the congress for the Comintern, was just forty. Yet they were deciding the fates and hopes of millions.

The congress began informally with Bukharin's interrogations of individual leaders. He was not harsh, but Zhou apparently blushed with embarrassment when questioned about his handling of military affairs. The congress then formally opened with a long, detailed report by Bukharin, who characterized the Chinese Communist party as still "growing up" and Comintern advisors as partly to blame for mistakes. But about the past, he concluded, "under the comparison of objective strengths, even given the correct strategy, we probably would have suffered a great defeat anyway.'' In other words, the Communist party had been too young and weak to prevent Chiang Kaishek's betrayal once he had set his mind on it. Bukharin offered some consolation, however. He reminded the delegates that the Bolsheviks themselves before their victory in 1917 had been defeated in 1905. He expressed his considered optimism that a similar Chinese success would not be delayed twelve years.

In the congress which followed, the mistakes of the past were identified and a new direction plotted. Emphasis was placed on careful preparation for a new revolutionary high tide which was bound to come. And a leadership to carry out this strategy was selected. Neither of the party's main founders were there—Li Dazhao had been killed by police the year before, and Chen Duxiu had remained home, in virtual retirement—so they were replaced by a true proletarian, Xiang Zhongfa, a barge worker and labor leader, who became the party's general secretary. Otherwise the political bureau remained much the same, since Bukharin emphatically endorsed experience and continuity as against those who demanded a whole new leadership team.

After the congress, most of the delegates returned to China immediately, but Zhou stayed on to attend the sixth Comintern congress and to resolve a controversy that throws an interesting sidelight on the times. During the period of Sino-Soviet cooperation, the Soviets had set up Sun Yatsen University in Moscow for the benefit of revolutionary Chinese students. In 1928, in the wake of the Chiang Kaishek coup and other political rivalries in the Soviet Union, allegations were made that there was an "antiparty" plot against the school's directors. Zhou was asked to investigate. After looking into the matter, he cleared all those who were charged, including Chiang Chingkuo, the son of Chiang Kaishek (and currently the president on Taiwan). The party's most hated enemy's son, who himself was not a party member, could still be trusted and endorsed as a revolutionary!

Back in China the new strategy scored successes. In less than two years, party membership in Shanghai alone grew to 3,000, despite the rigors of underground existence. (In comparison, in the spring of 1925, there had been only 1,000 members in the whole country.) In the countryside to the south, the Red Army established bases which counted their population in the millions. Meanwhile, the capitalist world was experiencing the first shocks of the 1929 stock-market crash, and Chiang Kaishek's opponents in the Nationalist party were lining up on the battlefield to unseat him. Could this be the long-awaited upsurge? The question was on everyone's lips.

Xiang Zhongfa, the party's general secretary, failed to take a decisive stand. Initiative passed to the director of propaganda, Li Lisan, the Hunanese student who had been the chief negotiator for the Shanghai strikers in 1925. Li answered with decision and in the affirmative. Revolution—indeed, world revolution—was imminent. And he initiated a party reorganization in response.

The Russians watched from afar in amazement. They had never really trusted Li, and thought he was too boastful. Even his Chinese comrades did not appreciate Li calling himself the "Lenin" of the Chinese party. But they were anxious for a revolutionary success in China. To get a balanced view of the situation, they asked Zhou Enlai to come to Moscow. The report Zhou made after his arrival confirmed Soviet suspicions. Li was going off half-cocked without the careful preparations they had advised earlier. Zhou, in contrast, impressed the Soviet leaders by his mature and balanced approach. Stalin praised him and invited him to speak before the Soviet party, a rare honor. In all, Zhou stayed on in Moscow several months. When he left at the end of the summer, Soviet leaders hoped he would return and take control of the Chinese party away from Li Lisan.

But when Zhou returned, it was too late. Li's ill-advised schemes had caused repeated disasters. Much of the party was up in arms demanding his removal. Red generals like Mao Zedong had simply stopped following his orders. A meeting of the central committee was held at the mountain resort of Lushan, where Zhou gave a famous report which aimed at restoring party unity by declaring Li's policies mistaken and ill-timed. In effect, he thereby supported Li's general policy, while eliminating the most obvious errors.

The so-called Li Lisan line was ended by this September 1930 meeting, but Li Lisan was still not out. It would take four more months and direct

ZHOU (THIRD FROM THE RIGHT) WITH OTHER RED COMMANDERS IN 1933.

intervention by the Russians before another central committee meeting was held and Li Lisan was shipped back to the Soviet Union for "reeducation." Zhou Enlai was disgraced for his handling of the affair and had to call on the entire party to "condemn my mistakes"—but he retained all his party posts. The new leaders, the "28 Bolsheviks," who had little experience outside of their Soviet training, could not afford to lose his talents.

The party's fortunes began to decline seriously after the installation of the new leaders. Some party members were angry that the inexperienced Bolsheviks were promoted instead of themselves or Zhou. But factional animosity paled in light of the long series of arrests and deaths that came in 1931. In mid-January a planning meeting for a Soviet congress was discovered, and the 23 arrested were shot two weeks later. The party thus lost some of its most promising young writers and experienced labor leaders. This was the work of the British police, who similarly had a hand in tracking down, from Hong Kong to Shanghai, the underground Comintern representatives in the Far East. This European couple, whose true identity remained in doubt, were not killed, but their papers provided clues that led to the arrests of numerous Communists, including the party's general secretary, Xiang Zhongfa, who was killed shortly after his arrest.

Possibly the most disastrous blow to the urban underground came with the arrest of Gu Shunzhang, the party's head of internal security, who was discovered quite by accident while masquerading as an itinerant magician. At first the party was able to cope. His family was immediately spirited away to prevent their use as hostages, and within hours the top echelons of the party in Shanghai went on alert. As time went on, however, the foreign and Chinese anti-Red squads closed in. Without Gu, who had close ties with the underworld, the party's defenses did not hold. According to Shanghai's French police, during the summer months of 1931 "several thousand" urban Communists were tried and executed by secret military tribunals.

Under a state of siege in the cities, the central committee decided to abandon them and head for the safer, Communist-dominated areas in the countryside. Toward the fall of 1931, Zhou Enlai took leave of his family in Shanghai. With a false beard and a long gown, he passed as a monk aboard a steamer heading south along China's coast. After reaching Fujian province, he disembarked and made the slow, careful journey inland.

In November 1931, while Zhou may still have been traveling to safety, the final scene of the grisly drama was played out. The Nationalist anti-Red squad captured a minor Communist known as "Stomach" Wang, who saved himself from execution by confessing to the slaughter of Gu Shunzhang's family. Wang alleged that Zhou Enlai ordered the massacre of the entire family in retaliation for Gu's defection to the Nationalists. He proved his claims by leading police to the burial site, where by some accounts as many as eleven bodies were dug up. Sensational news reports suggested that some had been buried alive. Zhou's alleged role received special prominence, since he was thought to be the head of the party at that time.

Without further evidence, these charges against Zhou can be dismissed as blatant propaganda. Gu Shunzhang, described as a defector, subsequently restored his ties to the Communist party and was executed by the Nationalists. "Stomach" Wang joined the anti-Red squad and later ran a garment factory. As for the bodies, an interesting sidelight on the matter came from Taiwan in the 1960s, when a lieutenant of the Shanghai gangland boss Du Yuesheng revealed that Du murdered the head of Shanghai's labor federation just before the April 12, 1927, coup by having him buried alive. Could the bodies have been just a few of the multitude of dead leftists? Internal police reports from the time, such as those of the French in Shanghai, reveal only a few suspected retaliatory murders, only thirty-five for the six years between 1928 and 1933, many of which are obviously not attributable to Zhou. Nevertheless, the charges against Zhou, regardless of their accuracy, do suggest the life-and-death struggle going on at that time and the dedication required to work underground. Zhou may have been happy to leave.

## SOVIET COMMANDER

Communist forces had survived best in the countryside. In the four years since the founding of the Red Army in 1927, Soviet areas had sprung up all over China, as revolutionary remnants of the peasant and workers' movements banded together with Communist armies. In classical bandit style, they situated their bases along the borders of several provinces. The Central Soviet, for example, straddled Jiangxi, Fujian, and Guangdong, just outside any one province's concern. Additionally, border areas were usually mountainous and less heavily populated, minimizing their importance and strengthening their defense. Thus protected, the Red Army grew to nearly 100,000 soldiers, and Soviet governments carried out agrarian policies affecting millions.

On November 7, 1931, the fourteenth anniversary of the Russian Revolution, representatives of the various Soviet areas gathered in Ruijin, a small mountain town near the Jiangxi-Fujian border, to elect a national Soviet government. The political commissar of the largest army, Mao Zedong, was made chairman of the government's executive committee. The military leader of that army, Zhu De, became chairman of the military council. The de facto power of these two leaders of the Red Army was now formally ratified.

Yet another chain of command existed in the party. Zhou Enlai, the head of the military affairs department for five years and more recently chief of the central bureau for Soviet affairs, represented the higher central authorities. When he arrived in Ruijin, one of his major tasks was to bring these local commanders under tighter central control.

The problem had first arisen in 1930, when the military leaders rebelled against Li Lisan. Later that year, Mao Zedong on his own authority arrested several thousand Communist activists on the pretext that they belonged to a secret "anti-Bolshevik" league. Many suspected that Mao had moved against them because of their continued allegiance to Li Lisan. Suspicions sparked a revolt, and for several months bloody fighting ensued between the hostile Communist camps.

Party leaders in Shanghai supported Mao but with qualifications. A report for Zhou's central Soviet bureau "found it hard to support the subjective conclusion that the incident was an anti-Bolshevik and liquidationist revolt," and suggested that "the incident was arbitrarily used to incriminate anyone as an anti-Bolshevik liquidationist." When Mao followed this report with mass trials,

Zhou realized he had to be on the scene to bring his refractory subordinate under control.

After his arrival, Zhou had no trouble persuading Zhu De, his old friend and the second most powerful man in the Soviet area, to denounce the excesses of the campaign against the "anti-Bolsheviks." The following February (1932), Zhou confronted Mao head-on at a military affairs conference, and convinced the officers in attendance that Mao's military strategy should be dropped and that instead of small guerrilla skirmishes the Red Army should launch major offensives. This solved the problem of Mao Zedong, whose political influence went into a decline, but left the much greater difficulty of Chiang Kaishek.

One factor in the growth of the Soviet areas was the relative inattention of Chiang Kaishek. He had been absorbed in defending himself against his Nationalist party rivals up through 1930, when a military victory against their combined forces guaranteed his single-handed control of the country. Though they were able to force him from office in 1931 over his handling of relations with Japan, they could not replace him; so his positions on that front were secure.

After subduing his fellow Nationalists, Chiang turned to the Communists. He renewed the white terror in the cities, and began a series of "encirclement and extermination" campaigns in the countryside. He modeled himself on, and followed the strategy of, the nineteenth-century Confucian general, Zeng Guofan, responsible for eliminating the Taiping peasant rebels. Chiang expected a similar victory.

Chiang's campaigns went on for several years, with success constantly eluding him. The first campaigns crumbled under guerrilla sniping. But as they failed and other problems arose, Chiang became obsessed with eliminating the Communists. To demands that he turn his attention to the Japanese, he replied that the Japanese were only a disease of the skin, but the Communists were a "disease of the heart." To guarantee their final demise, he massed an army of a million men, encircled the central Soviet area with a string of concrete blockhouses connected by barbed wire, and tried to strangle the economic life of the area while his troops pushed inward.

"TO THE FRONT," A WOODCUT, CAPTURES THE DO–OR–DIE SPIRIT DOMINATING THE DEFENSE OF THE SOVIET AREAS.

THE LUDING BRIDGE TODAY. THE LONG MARCHERS HAD TO FIGHT THEIR WAY ACROSS.

A CONTEMPORARY ARTIST'S VIEW OF THE LONG MARCHERS CROSSING THROUGH SWAMPLANDS.

Under the constant pounding of Chiang Kaishek's superior troops and weaponry, the Communists' frontal drives faltered. A recruiting drive used the slogan ''victory or death,'' but many, including Zhou Enlai, doubted if that represented any choice. So as the noose tightened, plans were made for a retreat. All the commanders knew they would have to break out of the encirclement if they continued to lose. The question was, when should they make the move?

Mao Zedong, still holding to his guerrilla strategy of never confronting overwhelming forces, argued strongly for getting out as soon as possible. Otto Braun, a German Communist sent by the Comintern as a military advisor, criticized Mao as ''conservative'' and ''pessimistic.'' Braun continued to press for one more big battle. Zhou Enlai went along with the majority, which sided with Braun. During the summer of 1934, the Red Army fought a series of defensive battles to hold their Jiangxi base, while Mao remained isolated in a small town sixty miles from Ruijin, suffering from malaria, according to some, and under house arrest, according to others.

The turning point came that fall when Zhou Enlai, Zhu De, and a third person went to visit Mao. After reviewing the situation with him, they finally agreed that retreat could wait no longer. The decision made, Zhou then went to Braun and the other commanders. They reluctantly conceded that Zhou was right and that it was time to go. Within weeks, the incredible trek across China known as the Long March would begin.

## THE LONG MARCH

Deception, luck, and six weeks of hard fighting brought the Red Army out of Chiang's encirclement and as far west as the mountainous and isolated province of Guizhou. After seizing the town of Zunyi by a stratagem of having Red soldiers pose as local troops and ask that the city's gates be opened, two dozen or more military and party leaders met in a two-story brick and tile building to assess their situation. Their decisions at the Zunyi Conference would have a major impact on their fate and that of the revolution.

A SKETCH MADE BY A LONG MARCH PARTICIPANT SHOWING A CAMP SITE IN THE GRASSLANDS.

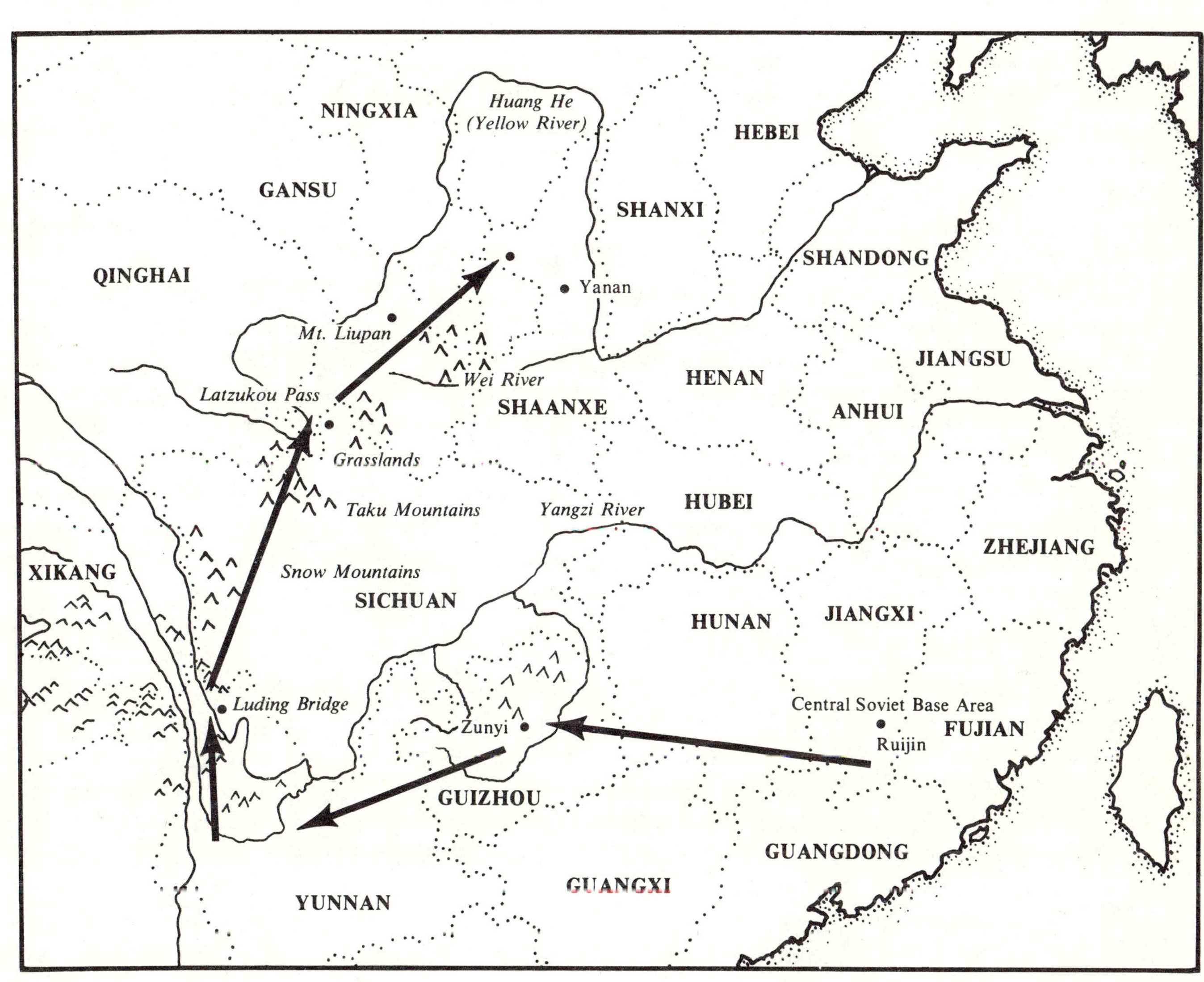


ZHOU'S ROUTE ON THE LONG MARCH.

At issue were the disasters of 1934. Until then Chiang's pressures had been withstood. Afterward he not only forced a retreat but hammered hard at the Red Army on the march. Possibly as many as half the Red soldiers that set out had been lost to enemy attacks and the rugged terrain. What went wrong and, more importantly, what was to be done?

Bo Gu, the young Russian-trained party general secretary, chaired the meeting, but Zhou Enlai, who gave the keynote address, set the tone. As in the past, Zhou was the first to admit his own mistakes, and he now publicly recognized the errors that brought about the retreat.

The floodgates of pent-up criticism were now open. Generals who suffered from decreased mobility during the first leg of the march condemned the policy of bringing along unnecessary supplies. The most thoroughgoing criticism, however, came from Mao Zedong, who lambasted the overall deviation from the earlier successful guerrilla strategy. He argued that Zhou's call for a "general attack" had not produced more than "general resistance," that the slogan, "Don't yield a single inch of Soviet territory," might have been politically correct, but was a military failure.

Zhou accepted the criticism. Bo Gu, to the contrary, tried to avoid responsibility for recent failures by pointing to earlier successes. Otto Braun, perhaps most responsible for strategy during the defeats, continued to defend his policies.

The conference supported Mao. The final report was subtitled "A Review of the Military Errors of Comrades Bo Gu, Zhou Enlai, and Li De (i.e. Otto Braun)." Bo Gu lost the post of general secretary. Mao replaced Zhou Enlai as chief poltical commissar and head of military affairs. Otto Braun lost his influence as an advisor. But although Mao advanced militarily and politically, Zhou still retained his power in the party's political bureau and continued to do much of the political and military planning. In the end, his admission of mistakes strengthened rather than weakened him. Like the jujitsu master, he rolled with the punches and turned them to his advantage.

Under the new leadership, the Long March continued. Still with great difficulty. After Zunyi the Red Army headed further west and then turned north, just avoiding major battles with Chiang Kaishek's troops and skirting the Himalaya massif.

The feats of heroism were legendary. Blocked by a length of the Yangzi river where the Taiping peasant rebels had been destroyed in 1864, the army trusted its fate to a suicide squad of 22 men who fought their way across a chain-link bridge whose planking had been torn up by the opposing troops. With a raging torrent rushing below and machine guns firing from above, the squad slowly and incredibly advanced. The bridge's defenders panicked and fled, but only after setting their fortifications and the far end of the bridge on fire. Caught between the flames and defeat, the young men of the squad plunged through the blaze to secure the bridge and save the day for the entire army. Such acts of bravery are few in military annals.

Nor was heroism limited to small groups under fire. The entire army advanced against incredible odds. In sight of Tibet, they crossed China's own Great Snow Mountains, where the poorly clad soldiers would collapse in the deep snow and die from exposure and exhaustion before their comrades could pick them up. In a foul, endless swamp known as the Grasslands, soldiers marched single file, holding a guide rope so that they did not sink and disappear in the treacherous mud. When no solid ground could be found for bivouacking, the troops slept standing up, back to back, with only exhaustion overcoming their fear of sinking into the morass. These areas were only two of many terrible obstacles, which included hostile tribes, supply shortages, and the obvious difficulty of a 6,000-mile, year-long march.

Zhou Enlai shared the hardships of the troops, as did all the leaders. He marched along with them during the day and then spent much of the evening poring over maps to plot the next day's route. Yet he still found time to talk to ordinary soldiers. One evening, for example, while out strolling deep in thought, he forgot to answer with the password when a sentry challenged him. The sentry recognized him, so there was no problem. But the incident got the two men talking, and Zhou invited the soldier to come sit by his fire when he was off duty. He did come, and their conversation lasted well into the night.

Many soldiers remembered such acts of kindness and attention; they also recalled Zhou's stern

ZHOU ENLAI, JUST AFTER THE LONG MARCH.

self-discipline. His orderlies experienced frequent embarrassment because of his refusal to bend the rules. Once when they prepared him an unusual meal of eggs, he asked to see the peasant from whom they had bought them. After some hemming and hawing, they were forced to admit they found the eggs in an abandoned hut. The eggs could not be returned, but Zhou demanded that a letter of apology be written and left, along with some money to pay for the eggs. Zhou believed that taking the eggs amounted to theft and would have made the Red Army just like warlord troops, which thought nothing of looting peasant villages. Similarly, Zhou once sat under a tree of fully ripened pears without eating even one. He told his aides he would not take one when he could not pay the owner.

One poor aide, a young fellow named Wei, was twice criticized by Zhou for his misguided good intentions. Wei's difficulties all began when, after some misgivings, he was elected to head the party cell which included Zhou Enlai. The cell was the lowest level of the party and this cell, except for Zhou, consisted of ordinary soldiers. Wei did not think Zhou had time for its meetings, and failed to notify him when the first meeting was held; so when Zhou asked when the meeting would be, Wei answered that it was already past. Zhou sharply reprimanded Wei and reminded him that he (Zhou) was still just an ordinary party member with the same responsibility for attending meetings. Wei chagrined, learned that lesson, but fell afoul of Zhou later when, once again trying to be helpful, he paid Zhou's party dues for him. Zhou took him aside for the second time and explained that he was an ordinary party member and had to pay his own dues. Perhaps Wei should not have been criticized, but Zhou was right in stressing that the party leaders should be treated equally and not given special treatment.

As one might suspect, Zhou received as well as gave criticism. At a time when the whole army was traveling largely on will power and sickness was taking its toll, an orderly delivering some medicine asked Zhou when the Long March would end. Zhou, perhaps a bit feverish, responded with a lecture about the propaganda value of the march and implied that they should stay on the road as long as possible. The orderly politely disagreed, and suggested that, if only for Zhou's health, an early end was preferable. Zhou laughed and recognized that the orderly was right.

The stern discipline and egalitarian values were necessary to hold the Red Army together through the test of the Long March. Many did not survive, and those who did paid a price. Zhou Enlai collapsed along the way and had to be carried by stretcher before he was well enough to complete the march on horseback. Deng Yingchao, his wife, contracted tuberculosis and later needed a long convalescent period. Mao Zedong's wife was wounded by schrapnel and had to leave their two small children behind with a peasant family. (Years later the children could not be found.) The list of such hardships is endless.

However, the Long March finally reached the barren northwest province of Shaanxi in October 1935. The main body of the Red Army now joined local units in control of a small Soviet area. Struggle would continue, but for the 5,000 weary survivors of the Long March, the sight of their comrades could not have been more welcome. The ordeal was over.

# 1935–1949

It was a tense moment for the American journalist traveling through the no-man's land between the Communist and Nationalist lines. Word had reached his adolescent Communist guide that the local anti-Communist militia had a Caucasian commander. Did the boy think that he, the only white man for hundreds of miles, was really the militia chief? If so, what would he do? The heavy local accent presented an almost insuperable barrier to communication.

A thin young officer appeared. Wearing the common shapeless uniform, but with an unusually thick and long black beard, he took command. "Hello. Are you looking for somebody?" The highly relieved Edgar Snow answered by introducing himself to Zhou Enlai.

Snow at this time was a minor figure on the Chinese scene. Raised in the United States, he wound up in China during a trip around the world financed by lucrative ventures into the booming stockmarket of the 1920s. A sharp-witted American editor in Shanghai recognized Snow's potential, and offered him a job as a roving reporter. Most Western journalists clung to the safety of the foreign enclaves in the port cities, but Snow roamed the interor at will, sending back pictures and vivid accounts of his travels. In 1935 he was stationed in Beijing, where the ties he developed to the progressive student movement provided him with an introduction to the Communists isolated in the northwest. In 1936 he set out for no-man's land to bring their story back to the English-speaking world.

Zhou Enlai was the first Communist leader Snow met. Describing him as being "as much a legend as a man," Snow expected this "scholar turned insurrectionist" to be a fanatic with a "fatal gleam" in his eye. But conversation revealed only a quiet, thoughtful army officer making his duty rounds. Snow described Zhou this way: "He was of slender stature, of medium height, with a slight wiry frame, boyish in his appearance despite his long black beard, and with large, warm, deep-set eyes. There was a certain amount of magnetism about him that seemed to derive from a curious combination of shyness, personal charm, and complete assurance of command. His English was somewhat hesitant and difficult, but it was understandable."

After their meeting on the trail, Snow left Zhou and continued on to the Communist headquarters in Baoan, where he met Mao Zedong, Zhu De, and other "legendary" leaders. The record of his travels, *Red Star Over China,* first published in 1937, introduced them to the world and for the first time made known that Zhou had organized the 1927 Shanghai insurrection. From this point on, Malraux's fictional Kyo Gisors became identified with Zhou, although Malraux himself never said whether Zhou was the model for his existential hero.

Translated into Chinese, Snow's book had a major impact on the informational blockade which the Chiang government had erected around the Communist forces. This overview of the personalities and activities of the previously isolated and underground movement won many adherents to the Communist cause. However, by 1937 and 1938, when the book and the translation became available, political developments in the northwest had already shaken the Nationalist order and fostered a new receptivity to the Communist message.

## "CHINESE DON'T FIGHT CHINESE"

After the Long March, the Communist forces were bottled up in the rugged terrain north of the Yangzi and west of the Taihang mountains. The easiest way out went through the Wei valley and then to the northern Chinese plains, the very route followed by the Zhou dynasty millennia earlier, when they conquered the Shang to lay the foundations of a distinctive Chinese culture. Now their ancient capital had become a sleepy provincial outpost of Xian, hosting Nationalist troops with the sole purpose of restraining, then eliminating the Red Army.

Zhou Enlai directed the propaganda war against these troops during that first bitter winter after the Long March. The simple message, "Chinese don't fight Chinese," encapsulated the strategy of a united front upon which the Communist party had decided in August 1935. To give the message poignancy, Deng Yingchao, Zhou's wife, led a woman's propaganda corps up to the front lines to

EDGAR SNOW.

IN DECEMBER 1935, THE STUDENTS OF BEIJING SPARKED A NEW PATRIOTIC MOVEMENT OF RESISTANCE TO JAPAN. HERE THEY HAVE JUST SEIZED A FIRE HOSE FROM POLICE, WHO HAD TRIED TO USE IT TO DISPERSE THEM.

THE MANCHURIAN TROOPS OF ZHANG XUELIANG.

"THE TIGER OF MANCHURIA," ZHANG ZUOLIN, NOT LONG BEFORE THE JAPANESE KILLED HIM BY BLOWING UP HIS TRAIN.

ZHANG XUELIANG (ON LEFT) ALSO MET IN XIAN WITH CHIANG KAISHEK'S PERSONAL ADVISOR, THE
AUSTRALIAN W. D. DONALD.

ZHOU IN EARLY 1937, PROBABLY IN YANAN.

shout the message across to soldiers in the opposing trenches. To give it substance, meager food supplies were shared with the Nationalist troops after word of a supply shortage came. By spring, relations on the front lines had warmed along with the weather.

But troops in trenches do not give orders. That summer battles were fought to test the Communist's strength. They won handily, then used their victory to sue the Nationalists for peace. Zhou asked a captured officer to deliver a personal letter to the commander on the other side. In it Zhou wrote, "Chinese don't fight Chinese. Inhuman is he who slays his own brother to feed the wolf."

Zhang Xueliang's eyes misted over as he read the letter addressed to him. He had good reason to heed Zhou's message. In 1928 Japanese assassins blew up the train his father, "the Tiger of Manchuria," was riding in. Command then passed to the son, but the "Young Marshal," as he was known in deference to his father, was no match for the continued Japanese onslaught. In 1931 they turned Manchuria into the puppet state of Manchukuo and forced Zhang to flee along with his troops. Chiang Kaishek then sent them to the northwest to fight the Communists and to isolate them from the patriotic movement demanding resistance against Japan.

Zhou Enlai understood the Young Marshal's story very well, and had contacts with some of the officers whom he knew from his own childhood in Manchuria. Once the Young Marshal showed himself to be receptive, Zhou quickly arranged private discussions to negotiate a ceasefire. By the fall of 1936, in the northwest at least, Chinese were not fighting Chinese.

Chiang Kaishek was still left to contend with. Ramrod straight in posture and purpose, he confided to his diary that he expected to "destroy the remnant Red bandits in a couple of weeks, or at most a month." To guarantee his final victory, he came to Xian in December 1936 to assume personal command of the final campaign.

The month before, Zhang and Chiang had argued in the Yellow River town of Luoyang over the arrest of leaders of the patriotic movement. The Young Marshal compared Chiang's behavior to that of the discredited warlords of years past. The Generalissimo curtly replied, "That is merely your viewpoint. I am the Government. My action was that of a revolutionary." Now in Zhang's territory, with his own crack troops and secret police flooding Xian, Chiang was rumored to be preparing further arrests. But Zhang moved first.

At 10:00 P.M. on December 11, Zhang met with other commanders and officers to resolve on a "military remonstrance," in effect, a mutiny designed to force a commander to respect his subordinate officers' wishes. Within hours the Manchurian troops seized the city and arrested Chiang, headquartered at a nearby hot springs resort. But having seized command, Zhang was at a loss to decide what to do next.

Chiang Kaishek retained his arrogance throughout the incident. Found in a bathrobe and without shoes or his false teeth in the hills behind his lodgings, he thought nothing of giving commands to his captors. A broad-backed captain carried him down from the hills. When the captain asked why Chiang would not fight the Japanese, Chiang snapped, "I am the leader of the Chinese people. I represent the nation. I think my policy is correct." This recalcitrance did not diminish in the face of the Young Marshal's pleas. In desperation Zhang sent his personal plane to Communist headquarters to bring back Zhou Enlai.

Word of the incident came first. There was great jubilation at the thought of a detested enemy finally getting his just deserts. Mao Zedong, by some reports, thought Chiang should be given a public trial and hanged. After some consideration, however, the Communists recognized Chiang's importance to the national united front and the divisive effect his death would have. When Zhou Enlai flew to Xian, instead of a sword he carred an olive branch, an eight-point plan for national unity.

Representing the ad hoc "Xian Emergency Committee," Zhou met with Chiang for the first time since Zhou had served as Chiang's military subordinate in Guangdong ten years before. No friendship was renewed. Chiang sullenly persisted in his refusal to consider any other opinion than his own. For more than a week and half, the committe met with Chiang but failed to budge him.

Meanwhile the situation grew critical. Moscow and Tokyo exchanged barbs, each seeing the other as the hidden plotter behind the scenes. The Manchurian soldiers lost patience, and support spread

ZHOU (IN AVIATOR'S CAP), WITH MAO ZEDONG TO HIS RIGHT, JUST BEFORE HIS DEPARTURE FOR XIAN.

ZHOU IN XIAN IN 1937, DURING THE NEGOTIATIONS FOR A UNITED FRONT. ON THE LEFT IS HIS FELLOW COMMUNIST, YE JIANYING, AND IN THE CENTER IS THE NATIONALIST PARTY REPRESENTATIVE, ZHANG ZHONG.

MAO ZEDONG AND ZHOU ENLAI OUTSIDE A YANAN CAVE HOUSE IN 1937.

ONCE THE WAR BEGAN, ZHOU MOVED TO NATIONALIST-CONTROLLED
AREAS TO COORDINATE THE UNITED FRONT. THIS IS HIS FORMAL
PORTRAIT FROM THAT TIME, 1938.

OPPOSITE PAGE: AFTER DENG YINGCHAO JOINED ZHOU IN HANKOU,
THEY WERE ABLE TO ENTERTAIN MANY OF THEIR OLD FRIENDS. HERE
THEY ARE WITH EDGAR SNOW.

for Chiang's execution. Chiang's own subordinates were preparing a rescue attempt, and many believed General He Yingqin would use the opportunity to eliminate Chiang and then replace him.

Zhou went sleepless for a week trying to resolve the matter. Young Marshal Zhang was weakening in his resolve to hold Chiang. An unconditional release would spell victory for the anti-Communist cause. Chiang's death, on the other hand, meant the dashing of any hopes for national unity. Zhou gambled upon a compromise settlement. Chiang was released without a formal agreement, thereby saving face and allowing him to deny he submitted to duress, but negotiations were to continue. With this understanding, Chiang Kaishek was allowed to fly out of Xian on Christmas day 1936.

Two weeks later, the announcement came that the anti-Communist drive was called off. The gamble had worked. Pressure was now off the Communists, who were able to establish larger, more permanent quarters in the town of Yanan. A united front was at least in the works, though the negotiations proceeded slowly. The only casualty of the incident turned out to be the Young Marshal. As proof of his sincerity he accompanied Chiang on his departure from Xian. He was then put under house arrest and not released until Chiang's death forty years later. His troops blamed Zhou for this—and indeed threatened his life because of it—but it was only the final coda of Zhang's own strange tale.

### LIFE IN THE YANAN YEARS

From 1937 to 1947 the Communist capital of Yanan represented an island of peace in a world at war. A relatively inaccessible small town, it served more as a spiritual center than as a unified command post for the vast network of Communist guerrilla bases throughout the northern Chinese countryside. The Japanese left it alone during the war, and the Communists seized this opportunity to develop their ideas on politics and social organization. Most of Mao Zedong's published writings come from this period, and many scholars consider the experiences of the Yanan years, especially the enforced ascetic self-reliance, to be the source of the unique Chinese form of Communism.

But although many other top leaders settled down in Yanan, Zhou kept on the move. He did not expect this at first. In fact, Deng Yingchao took great pains to furnish their lodgings in Yanan as comfortably and artistically as possible. The cave house they were assigned had paper windows on which Deng planned to write their favorite poems—until she was advised that the poems' black characters would block out all heat and light. But the cave house saw little use in the early war years, as Zhou moved from city to city as the Communists' chief representative and negotiator.

At first, in early 1937, Zhou spent much time in Xian, still working out the details of the truce with Chiang Kaishek. Then in July, after the Japanese attacked Beijing, Zhou rushed to the southeastern mountain resort of Lushan to pressure Chiang for further national unity. As northern China and then the Yangzi valley fell to the Japanese, Zhou retreated with the Nationalists, first to the central China city of Hankou and then to the southwestern city of Chongqing, in mountainous Sichuan province. Deng joined him in Hankou and accompanied him to Chongqing, the wartime Nationalist capital, where they lived together during most of the war years.

They were trying times. Officially Zhou was no longer a hunted outlaw hiding underground, but the representative of a Chinese organization formally recognized by the government. Nevertheless, Zhou was treated at best like the ambassador of an unfriendly foreign country. All his movements were observed. Cars followed him whenever he went out. And he had to assume that everything he said was overheard. Despite these circumstances, Zhou still functioned as an able propagandist for the Communist cause. He was particularly effective with the foreign press, who appreciated his modest charm and honesty.

Even trying circumstances have their limits, and these were reached in Chongqing in early 1941. By then more than three years of fighting had brought the war to a standstill. Throughout much of China the Japanese controlled the cities and railways, while Chinese guerrillas ruled the countryside. The Eighth Route and New Fourth armies were

ZHOU CAUGHT BY PHOTOGRAPHER ROBERT CAPA IN A MORE  INFORMAL POSE.

ZHOU BROKE HIS ARM WHILE RIDING A HORSE, AND WHEN IT DID NOT HEAL PROPERLY, HE HAD TO GO
TO THE SOVIET UNION FOR MEDICAL TREATMENT. HERE HE IS BEING WELCOMED BACK TO YANAN IN
THE SPRING OF 1940 BY MAO ZEDONG AND OTHER COMMUNIST LEADERS.

ZHOU ADDRESSING RALLY, 1939.

ZHOU LED THE COMMUNIST PARTY LIAISON GROUP IN CHONGQING DURING THE WAR. HERE HE IS SEEN READING THE PAPER IN THE PARTY'S OFFICE.

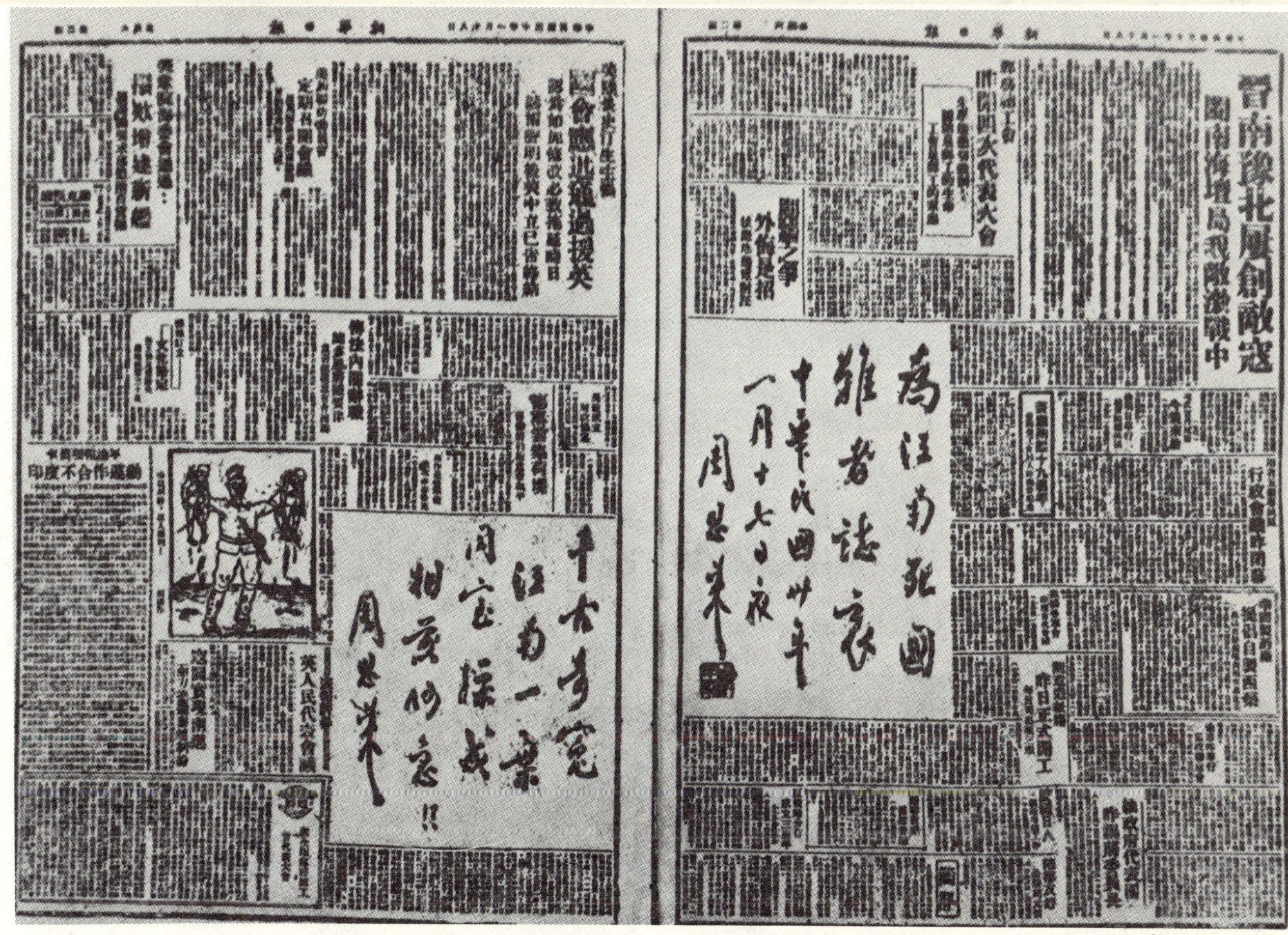

*THE NEW CHINA DAILY NEWS,* JANUARY 18, 1941. ZHOU'S POEM IS IN THE INSET ON THE LEFT. THE THREE CHARACTERS IN THE LINE ON THE LEFT ARE HIS NAME .

LARGER FORCES HELPED TO PRESERVE SOME SEMBLANCE OF THE UNITED FRONT. HERE WORKERS
COLLATE A MAGAZINE UNDER THE BENEVOLENT GAZES OF ROOSEVELT AND STALIN.

especially strong, since they were formerly units of the Red Army and experienced guerrilla fighters. But Chiang ordered the New Fourth Army to withdraw from the area it occupied south of the Yangzi and then, on January 4, 1941, troops loyal to him attacked the New Fourth Army headquarters and killed its commander, General Ye Ting. Only 1,000 survived, out of an original 9,000 composed largely of wounded soldiers, medical personnel, and political cadre. National unity was sundered by this inexplicable move, and Zhou Enlai had to respond.

In Chongqing the Communists ran a newspaper, the *New China Daily News,* subject to the same censorship as the other papers. Chiang's government refused to allow any news of the incident to be printed. Zhou skirted the censors by having two issues printed, one for them and one for public distribution. But there was a greater political problem. Even if Chiang was willing to destroy wartime unity, the Communists still wanted to retain the united front. Even limited cooperation reduced Chiang's attacks on them. But, more importantly, they saw the united front as the only sure way of uniting the Chinese people against the common enemy, Japan. Chiang might prefer civil war, but the Communists were fighting in a world war. So how could Zhou get past the censors and take a position on the incident, yet not destroy the united front? He did it with a poem.

In his own calligraphy, he wrote a poem entitled ''In Grief for the National Martyrs South of the River.'' In sixteen pithy characters arranged in the classical meter, Zhou wrote (in rough translation):

> ''An injustice rare for ancient times.
> South of the river, one leaf;
> In the same room, weapons raised.
> Why hurry to help cook!?''

To the uninformed the poem sounds like gibberish. But the Chinese knew that the one leaf (*ye*) south of the river was Ye Ting, commander of the New Fourth Army. And those who knew their classical history understood the last line, which paraphrased a similar poem, a story in itself.

According to legend, a particularly tyrannical and capricious emperor intended to kill his younger brother, but decided at the last moment to give the young man a final chance to save his life. If he could take seven steps and in that space of time compose a perfectly rhymed poem, his life would be spared. The brother took the steps, then delivered these lines:

> ''To cook the beans, the beanstalk is burnt.
> The beans inside the pot cry,
> 'We are both born of the same root.
> Why the great hurry to help cook?' ''

When the emperor heard these words, he broke down and released his brother.

Zhou may have hoped for a similar dramatic response to his plea that the beanstalk shouldn't help cook the beans or, more simply, that Chinese shouldn't fight Chinese. Yet even though he took to the street himself selling the newspaper, the message failed to reach, or affect, the highest circles of the Nationalist party. So although Zhou continued negotiations on the united front in Chongqing for two and half more years, the talks went nowhere. The united front was one of the casualties of the attack on the New Fourth Army.


## THE RISE OF MAO ZEDONG

In August 1943 Zhou returned to Yanan and a hero's welcome. He had ably represented the Communist cause and promoted national unity for nearly eight years. Now it was time for him to return to the inner party circles and advance a new type of unity.

At issue was the dissolution of the Comintern. For more than twenty years the Chinese Communist party had been an official branch of the Comintern. For the first fifteen of those, Comintern advisors played a major role in the party's life; the German Communist Otto Braun, for example, helped direct military affairs before the Long March. Since arriving in Yanan, the party had been acting independently, but it still had a formal connection. Now Stalin severed that.

Zhou welcomed the change. In his speech upon his return to Yanan, he said: ''After the dissolution of the Comintern, one thing should be made clear; that is, that the Chinese Communist party will be more responsible and independent to solve the problems of the Chinese revolution.'' He further specified the form that independence would take:

"Comrade Mao Zedong's ideas, throughout the entire history of the party, have developed into a Sinified Marxism-Leninism and are thus the line of Chinese Communism." In short, the authority of Stalin was to be replaced by that of Mao.

Zhou remained in the more hospitable climate of Yanan for more than a year while subordinates continued the fruitless negotiations with Chiang in Chongqing. Zhou returned to Chongqing twice more during the war, in late 1944 and early 1945, the first time with Patrick Hurley, the personal representative of President Roosevelt, who was concerned with uniting the feuding Chinese parties. But even the American president's intervention could not force Chiang to relinquish his supremacy or the Communists their independence. So Zhou remained in Yanan, where the party reorganization, the so-called Rectification Campaign, was going on; it would culminate in mid-1945 with the seventh party congress. Mao's ideological leadership was confirmed, and Zhou continued on as the second or third top man in the party.

At the war's end, an intensive effort was made to avert civil war. Mao Zedong and Zhou Enlai flew to Chongqing to negotiate directly with Chiang. In a significant gesture of goodwill, Mao even toasted his hated enemy who had killed most of his family. Much to the surprise of his audience, Mao raised his glass and offered in tribute, "Long live Generalissimo Chiang Kaishek." Along with some reductions in political demands such as settling for a preliminary political "conference" instead of an immediate coalition government, the six weeks of talks resulted in better relations and prevented the immediate outbreak of war.

But all was not quiet on the former battle fronts. Throughout northern China, Communist partisans rushed to disarm the defeated Japanese and replace them and their Chinese puppets. Chiang's troops, still isolated in the southwest, could not arrive until much later. When they did arrive, they would try to seize control, often from officials hastily elected in the interim. To prevent this, Chiang ordered the Japanese to remain in place and to surrender only to his men. With all these groups claiming authority, dispute was inevitable.

Washington once again intervened. General George Marshall, responsible for the American plan for Europe's postwar construction, came to China. Along with Zhou Enlai and a Nationalist party representative, Marshall formed a "Committee of Three" to supervise a ceasefire. Next came the formation of a multiparty Political Consulative Conference to draft a constitution. Additional agreements on the reduction and integration of armed forces led Marshall to consider his mission a success. On March 11 he returned to the United States to arrange a $500 million loan for China from the Export-Import Bank.

With Marshall gone, the "selfish irreconcilables" (Marshall's term for the Nationalist hawks) pressured Chiang into dispatching troops to Communist-dominated Manchuria. This action renewed the civil war and lost Chiang the strategic city of Changchun. A major counterattack regained the city in May. Marshall rushed back and forced a temporary truce, but it was too late. Chiang was convinced, he told Marshall, "it was first necessary to deal harshly with the Communists, and later, after two or three months, to adopt a generous attitude." The Communists, on the other hand, saw Marshall as ineffective at best, and an agent for the Nationalists at worst. Marshall's prestige plummeted. He returned to Washington, but not until he had condemned both sides, the Nationalist party for its "feudal control of China" and the Communist party for its "unwillingness to make a fair compromise."

Zhou Enlai, now back in Yanan, shifted from planning for peace to preparing for war. The Red Army was outnumbered three to one. During the second half of 1946, the Nationalist forces rolled up victory after victory, seizing 165 towns and 174,000 kilometers of territory. The Communist commanders, unsure of ultimate success, deserted Yanan. Dividing into two groups to minimize any potential losses, they set out on what has sometimes been called "the little Long March" through the hills of Shaanxi to elude their Nationalist pursuers.

After a year of fighting, the tide turned. Protests against Chiang's rule swept the cities and brought new recruits to the Communist armies, which grew to half the size of the Nationalists and scored their first advances in the summer of 1947. Later that year, Lin Biao initiated a campaign that cost Chiang half a million of his best troops by November 1948. At this point, the Communists achieved

ZHOU ENLAI IN YANAN, STANDING BEHIND MAO ZEDONG PHYSICALLY AND POLITICALLY.

THE WAR EFFORT: COMMUNIST TROOPS ON THE MARCH.

THE WAR EFFORT: THIS 1938 WOODCUT WAS CALLED "PROTECT OUR MOTHERLAND."

parity, and Nationalist troops began to defect en masse. At the battle of Huaihai, two entire divisions joined the Communist ranks. From September 1948 to January 1949, Chiang's government lost 1.5 million men. By June 1949, four million Red soldiers held the bulk of China in their hands. A massive popular victory had been won.

For Zhou Enlai, thirty years dedicated to the revolution—as student activist, military commissar, insurrectionist, underground organizer, Red commander, Long Marcher, united front negotiator, poet, and publicist—culminated in the desired end. But this was just a beginning: a quarter century as premier of the world's largest and most revolutionary state lay ahead.

THE WAR EFFORT: SUCCESSFUL TROOPS CELEBRATE

THE WAR EFFORT: ONE OF THE MOST SUCCESSFUL TECHNIQUES
AGAINST THE JAPANESE WAS "TUNNEL WARFARE."
HERE COMMUNIST SOLDIERS CLIMB OUT OF THEIR TUNNEL TO
LAUNCH A SURPRISE ATTACK.

ANOTHER ASPECT OF THE WAR EFFORT WAS LAND REFORM AND RENT REDUCTION. THIS WOODCUT CELEBRATES THE PEASANT'S NEW-FOUND PROSPERITY.

ZHOU'S CAREER IN INTERNATIONAL DIPLOMACY BEGAN DURING THE WAR. HERE IN 1943 HE MEETS WITH AMERICAN AND RUSSIAN MILITARY OFFICERS.

ZHOU ENLAI, PATRICK HURLEY, MAO ZEDONG, ZHANG ZHIZHONG OF THE NATIONALIST PARTY, AND ZHU DE, THE COMMUNIST MILITARY COMMANDER, IN YANAN DURING HURLEY'S VISIT.

ZHOU CONFERRING WITH MAO DURING THE SEVENTH PARTY CONGRESS.

ZHOU ENLAI AND ANNA LOUISE STRONG IN YANAN IN 1946. MS. STRONG WAS ONE OF A NUMBER OF AMERICANS SYMPATHETIC TO THE COMMUNIST CAUSE.

ZHOU SIGNS THE POSTWAR CEASEFIRE OF JANUARY 1946
WHILE GENERAL GEORGE C. MARSHALL OBSERVES.

ZHOU RETURNED TO YANAN AFTER SIGNING THE CEASEFIRE. HERE HE TALKS WITH ZHU DE AND MAO
ZEDONG, WHO CAME TO MEET HIS PLANE.

IN THE SUMMER OF 1946, ZHOU LIVED IN THE REESTABLISHED NATIONALIST CAPITAL OF NANJING.

ZHOU, MARSHALL, ZHU DE, ZHANG ZHIZHONG OF THE NATIONALIST PARTY, AND MAO ZEDONG DURING MARSHALL'S MARCH 1946 VISIT TO YANAN, JUST BEFORE HIS RETURN TO THE U.S.

AS THE NATION SLIPPED INTO CIVIL WAR, ZHOU WORKED TO RALLY THE SUPPORT OF THE INTELLIGENTSIA. HERE HE SPEAKS IN SHANGHAI ON THE TENTH ANNIVERSARY OF THE DEATH OF LU XUN, CHINA'S GREATEST MODERN WRITER.

OPPOSITE PAGE: MARSHALL'S NEGOTIATING EFFORTS FAILED TO STOP THE CIVIL WAR. HERE ZHOU IS ABOUT TO BOARD MARSHALL'S OWN PLANE TO RETURN TO YANAN FROM NANJING AFTER THE TALKS COLLAPSED. MARSHALL HIMSELF LEFT SOON AFTERWARD.

THIS WOODCUT, "JOINING THE ARMY," WAS USED TO APPEAL TO THE PEASANTS IN ALREADY LIBERATED AREAS IN 1947.

ZHOU PLOTTING STRATEGY DURING THE CIVIL WAR.

ZHOU ON THE MARCH AFTER THE EVACUATION OF YANAN.

COMMUNIST ARTILLERY ON THE ATTACK.

COMMUNIST TROOPS CROSSING THE YANGZI IN THE FINAL STAGE OF THE CIVIL WAR.

"UNITY IS STRENGTH," A WOODCUT PROMOTING ANTIGOVERNMENT DEMONSTRATIONS.

STUDENTS IN SHANGHAI DEMONSTRATING AGAINST THE GOVERNMENT IN 1948.

CHIANG KAISHEK (CENTER) MADE A LAST-MINUTE EFFORT TO RESTORE HIS SAGGING FORTUNES BY ENLISTING THE AID OF PHILIPPINE PRESIDENT, ELPIDIO QUIRINO (RIGHT). THE EFFORT FAILED.

ZHOU ENLAI REVIEWING TROOPS AS THE CENTRAL COMMITTEE ENTERS THE NEW CAPITAL OF BEIJING.

ZHOU STANDS BY AS THE FORMATION OF THE PEOPLE'S REPUBLIC OF CHINA IS ANNOUNCED.

1949–1965

On October 1, 1949, Mao Zedong announced the formation of the People's Republic of China with the stirring phrase, "We have stood up." The era of unequal treaties between China and its neighbors was now over. But it was Zhou Enlai who had to sit down the next day and start the painstaking process which established diplomatic relations with the rest of the world.

Zhou was the natural choice for foreign minister. He was fluent in several languages, had spent time abroad, and, most importantly, had already demonstrated substantial diplomatic skills during the war years. Only one thing could possibly disqualify him for the post: he was also the obvious candidate for prime minister. The task of building a government, almost from the ground up, required his administrative skills. But Zhou's dedication was such that he took on the back-breaking labor of both jobs, at least until 1958, when he handed over the foreign ministry to Chen Yi, a comrade of Zhou in Paris and a fighter with Mao in the Jinggang mountains. Even after 1958, Zhou still played a major role in foreign relations, by accompanying Chen Yi abroad and handling the most important negotiations at home.

To cope with these jobs, Zhou, now in his fifties, established a work style that he would follow to his very last days. Mornings and afternoons were given to meetings and conferences, where very often he would be the featured speaker. Evenings were available for state dinners, where diplomatic and other matters could be handled in a more relaxed setting. Then at night, when most people were content to retire, Zhou warmed up to the serious work of reading and writing reports or engaging selected guests in conversation. Lord Montgomery, the hero of North Africa in World War II, may have set a record when his talk with Zhou lasted *seven* hours, but conversations of three and four hours were not at all unusual.

By Western standards Zhou was a classic workaholic, but none of his guests perceived any of the tension or abruptness often associated with the hard worker. Zhou, in contrast, was always relaxed and attentive. Montgomery said of his talk with Zhou, "I enjoyed evey minute of it, and so, I fancy, did he."

Zhou extended a warm concern to the smallest details and to the unexpected. United Nations General Secretary Dag Hammerskjold on his visit to China was accompanied by a personal assistant who was suspected of being an American spy. Instead of isolating the young man, Zhou welcomed him. As he remarked later, "I knew that the American young man was only a plainclothesman; yet I paid him special attention. I kept him with us when the photographer took pictures of us, and assigned him a seat at the banquet. He was overwhelmed. We need not be afraid of American secret agents. On the contrary, we should work with them."

Yet Zhou did not share the politician's and diplomat's tendency to avoid controversy by obscuring the issue. He confronted issues head on, and clarified fine points of politics, without being brittle and dogmatic or trying to humiliate his interlocuter. When a group of American students visited China in 1957, one asked about "Communist China's" chances of entering the United Nations. Before answering the question, Zhou commented on the seemingly innocent choice of words:

"I would like first to correct this name. China's national name is 'The People's Republic of China,' just as America is called 'The United States of America.' We cannot call America 'Eisenhower's America' or 'Republican America.' That would be most inappropriate. Okay, Eisenhower leads America, but we can only say that America is under the leadership of Eisenhower or the Republican party, just as China is under the leadership of the Communist party. A country is the people's, and the people choose their representatives to lead their country. This thinking is not only held by the Chinese people; America's ancient sage Lincoln said it very well, 'A country should belong to its people.'"

Zhou's adroit allusions to American politics and history revealed his diplomatic skills along with his theoretical precision. Had he been fully able to employ them, modern history might have taken quite a different turn. Unfortunately that was not to be.

OPPOSITE PAGE: ZHOU ADDRESSES THE CHINESE PEOPLE'S POLITICAL CONSULTATIVE CONGRESS, THE BASE ON WHICH THE NEW GOVERNFMENT WAS BUILT.

1949
中國人民政治協商會議

A HAPPY MAO ZEDONG AND ZHOU ENLAI ENJOY
THEIR GOVERNMENTAL RESPONSIBILITIES.

ONE OF THE MANY STUDENT DELEGATIONS THAT
ZHOU HOSTED.

ONE OF ZHOU'S FIRST ACTS AS FOREIGN MINISTER WAS TO SIGN A TREATY OF FRIENDSHIP WITH THE SOVIET UNION, WHICH HE DOES HERE. STALIN AND MAO LOOK ON.

PHOTO ON PAGE 117: THE CHINESE DELEGATION TO THE GENEVA CONFERENCE OF 1954.

Midnight in Beijing, a year and day after Mao said, ''We have stood up.'' The new state's most serious foreign-policy crisis was about to explode unless Zhou could do something. As he sat in the foreign ministry waiting for the Indian ambassador, Zhou must have reviewed the evolution of the crisis.

The roots were sunk deep in the cold war between capitalism and socialism that had gone on since the 1917 Russian revolution. That war had entered a new and serious phase in the late 1940s, as the two giants, the United States and the Soviet Union, squared off over the postwar control of Europe.

For a while Asia seemed immune, because the local hostilities had a far different dynamic. Revolutionary nationalism represented forces distant from those of the industrialized states of Europe. Moreover, the United States had declared a hands-off policy. Secretary of State Dean Acheson on January 12, 1950, told the National Press Club, ''We must take the position we have always taken—that anyone who violates the integrity of China is the enemy of China and is acting contrary to our own interests.'' A month later the state department issued a statement removing any doubt that ''Formosa'' (Taiwan) was excluded or not a part of China.

Then the cold war came to Asia when a civil conflict erupted in Korea. Although this was an affair for the Koreans themselves, or for the Americans and Russians who had displaced the Japanese in 1945 (though by 1950 the Russian troops had gone), China was dragged into the conflict by President Truman, who, contrary to explicit remarks made months before, included Taiwan, still held by Chiang Kaishek, in the American defense perimeter and declared its occupation by Communist forces would be ''a direct threat to the security of the Pacific area and to United States forces.'' Zhou Enlai immediately denounced the action as ''aggression against the territory of China and a total violation of the United Nations charter.''

Zhou did not follow his sharp words with any immediate reaction. While the fighting seesawed in South Korea, China adopted a wait-and-see attitude. Only after massive American intervention restored the government of the unpopular Syngman Rhee and threatened to topple the government of North Korea did Zhou warn that the ''Chinese people absolutely will not tolerate foreign aggression, nor will they supinely tolerate seeing their neighbors savagely invaded.''

This was the situation that October night in 1950 as Zhou waited for Ambassador Pannikar of India. He then faced two options: to contain the conflict or to broaden it. The latter threatened a new world war, which this time would be fought with atomic bombs; but the former could pose an equally unacceptable threat to China and almost certain defeat for its North Korean friends. Zhou attempted a compromise of sorts. China would stay out of the fighting if the Americans did as well; that is, if American troops were kept below the 38th parallel. But if the Americans came north, China would send in troops as an act of self-defense. Zhou relied on Pannikar to deliver this message, since there was no direct diplomatic channel between the United States and China.

Zhou's efforts for a negotiated solution did not take into account American political realities. The Truman administration worked with one set of assumptions, but General MacArthur, the commander in the field, made his own independent judgments. The same day that Truman told a press conference that ''only South Korean troops would occupy the north frontier of Korea''—apparently in response to Zhou's diplomatic initiative—the *New York Times* reported that MacArthur's headquarters ''formally denied repeated reports that United Nations (American) forces would halt south of the Chinese Communist line . . . in an attempt to avoid possible international incidents.'' MacArthur's open threat to invade China left Zhou little choice. A week later Chinese and American troops clashed for the first time.

Cold-war hysteria now poisoned Sino-American relations. Six months after the fighting began, and only a little more than a year after the State Department declared the integrity of China to be in the American interest, a young State Department officer called territorial integrity ''an ironic phrase'' and then explained with rhetorical overkill that the authorities in Beijing were ''a colonial Russian government—a Slavic Manchukuo on a larger scale. It is not the Government of China. It does not pass the first test. It is not Chinese.'' The speaker, Dean Rusk, went on to preside over the American involvement in Vietnam, where he invoked similar arguments.

The fighting eventually ended, ironically with the same results that Zhou had proposed at the start: Korea remained divided along the 38th parallel. But Sino-American relations could not resume as before. Despite the dismissal of General MacArthur, the memory of the overt hostilities and of the more subtle wartime propaganda persisted.

A 1951 *Saturday Evening Post* article aptly conveys the sentiments of the times: ''They Tried to Make Our Marines Love Stalin:...nineteen American fighting men who were prisoners... weren't beaten or starved—but the propaganda torments they went through would curl your hair.'' The accent was not on the positive, on the protection which Chinese soldiers gave to the captured Marines assaulted by angry Korean civilians, but on the negative, on the ''brainwashing'' sessions in which the Chinese tried to pass on their own revolutionary convictions. For more than a decade, scholarly articles and popular magazines would develop the theme of thought control, until China was widely perceived as a colony of mindless ''blue ants'' living in a ''slave society'' ruled by leaders who were certifiably insane.

The Taiwan problem also stems from this period. Originally ''a refugee on a small island off the coast of China with the remnant of his forces'' from whom the Chinese people had ''completely'' withdrawn their support (according to Secretary of State Acheson), Chiang Kaishek was transmogrified into the ruler of all China. In a world where the Beijing authorities were not Chinese, Taiwan could become all of China. The country without a government was complemented by a government without a country.


## THE SPURNED HANDSHAKE

Korea made diplomacy immeasurably more difficult. Before the conflict only three major countries, the Soviet Union, Great Britain, and India, had recognized China. More than twenty smaller countries, including the new state of Israel,

joined them, but diplomatic recognition from another large state would not come until 1964, when France established relations. The People's Republic would be excluded from the United Nations until 1971.

For Zhou Enlai and the other Communists, diplomatic isolation came with no surprise. Red China, with its capital in Yanan during the war, had been ignored and established a pattern of self-sufficiency. The People's Republic, far larger and more resourceful, could surely survive. So Zhou proceeded to apply the lessons learned in the war years. He practiced ''people's diplomacy.'' If heads of state were inaccessible, ordinary people could still be reached. From the early 1950s on, China became the site of innumerable conferences of youth and intellectuals who braved government disfavor to practice people-to-people friendships and, inevitably, to meet with Zhou Enlai.

Meanwhile, slow gains were made in formal diplomatic circles. The 1954 Geneva conference provided a showcase for Zhou Enlai's formidable negotiating talents, when the foreign ministers from all the major countries met for three months to work out a comprehensive solution to the crisis in southeastern Asia. Zhou's personal efforts and magnetism were credited by both the French and the Vietnamese with contributing significantly to the final accord. And it was in Geneva that an incident occurred which symbolized Sino-American relations and, perhaps, foretold the fate of the settlement reached at the conference.

It was a July morning toward the end. Zhou Enlai arrived early at the Palais des Nations. Noticing the fine murals in the Grand Salle, he paused to study them more closely. While his back was turned, the American delegation entered, headed by Secretary of State John Foster Dulles, a tall, forbidding puritan known for his crusading anticommunism and his recent remark that he would meet Zhou Enlai privately ''only if our cars collide in the street.'' When Zhou heard the group approaching, he turned and offered his hand in friendship. Dulles looked him in the face, frowned, then ostentatiously withdrew his hands behind his back before proceeding on.

Dulles refused to sign the final accord reached at Geneva. As a result, without American backing, free elections were never held. The ''temporary''

REPUBLIQUE POPULAIRE
DE CHINE

ZHOU ENTERING THE GENEVA CONFERENCE.

ZHOU ADDRESSING THE BANDUNG CONFERENCE OF 1955.

ZHOU SEES THE SIGHTS IN INDIA, 1954.

IN 1956 HE DONS A PAKISTANI TURBAN.

division of Vietnam hardened into a national boundary. Fighting resumed in 1960, and the United States sent in ''advisors'' to protect South Vietnam from the ''Chinese'' threat. A single handshake could not have stopped this process, but it could have opened the way toward an effective negotiated settlement.

What the United States spurned, the Third World welcomed. Soon after Geneva, Zhou's offer of China's friendship was accepted by the delegates from 29 African and Asian nations gathered in Bandung, Indonesia, to express what Prime Minister Nehru of India called their ''new dignity'' in the emerging international order and their refusal to be dragged into European or American disputes.

Chinese success at Bandung came very much from Zhou's own personal effort. He had come with a prepared speech, but scrapped it after noticing an undercurrent of fear and doubt about China's revolutionary politics. During the mid-afternoon break, just hours before his scheduled appearance, Zhou totally revamped his address. The delegates were all listening intently when he began to speak:

''The Chinese delegation has come to seek unity and not to start arguments. We Communists have never concealed our belief in communism and consider socialism to be best. But, at this meeting, it would be foolhardy to propagate individual ideologies or national political systems....''

This is what the delegates wanted to hear. Differences were recognized, but unity could be achieved. More than anyone else, Zhou Enlai emerged as the symbol of ''the Bandung spirit,'' especially when he enunciated five principles of nonintervention and peaceful coexistence. Zhou even became something of a popular hero, and his car was mobbed by enthusiastic crowds hoping to catch a glimpse of him.

The Bandung principles and Zhou's behavior there considerably lessened international fears, prompted by the United States, that China was a dangerous diplomatic outlaw. Nepal, Egypt, Syria, and Yemen recognized the People's Republic. Indonesia signed an important accord on dual nationality. Prime ministers of a number of Asian countries came to visit China, and Zhou reciprocated with a tour of southern and southeastern Asia in 1956.

Zhou even extended the hand of friendship to the United States again. In May 1955 he expressed his willingness to negotiate on the ''question of relaxing tension in the Taiwan area,'' and for the first time referred to ''the liberation of Taiwan by peaceful means so far as it is possible.'' But this only led to inconclusive talks in Warsaw. Secretary of State Dulles was just then practicing ''brinksmanship''—''the ability to get to the verge without getting into war''—and negotiated solutions did not fit into his plans. When the Chinese followed up with an offer to allow American correspondents to travel to China, the State Department refused to issue valid passports. The hand of friendship remained spurned.


## ''ORDINARY WORKER''

As the sun rose that June morning in 1958, no clouds dimmed its luster or softened its rays as they poured down on the ragged line of middle-aged intellectuals seeking protection under their broad-brimmed straw hats. They had just marched from Beijing to a suburban construction site where a dam was being built. As they approached, a worker rushed out.

''We welcome the administrators who...''

But before he could finish, he was interrupted. ''There are no administrators here, nor any premiers, ministers, department heads, or that sort of thing. Here everybody is an ordinary worker.''

The ''ordinary worker'' speaking was none other than Premier Zhou Enlai.

Zhou had been to the site just weeks before, along with Mao Zedong, Zhu De, and other top party leaders. They came for the day to set an example for lower-level administrators, who were all supposed to engage in some manual labor. This was not only good for their own health, but intended as part of a larger process to break down distinctions between mental and manual labor, and between the leaders and the led. Zhou, Mao, and the others worked hard that day, but when it was all done Zhou was unhappy. As he surveyed the results, he remarked, ''We've done so little. When will the dam ever be finished?''

Now Zhou had returned with a large contingent of cadre fresh from their offices. Their average age

BUREAUCRATS GOING TO WORK WITH ZHOU IN THE LEAD.

ZHOU PASSING ALONG BASKETS OF DIRT.

SOME OF THE MANUAL LABOR WAS MORE
CEREMONIAL. HERE ZHOU AND FOREIGN
MINISTER CHEN YI TRY HAMMERING HOT STEEL.

PUSHING A WHEELBARROW.

MASSIVE NEW CONSTRUCTION PROJECTS WERE FINISHED DURING THE GREAT LEAP FORWARD. HERE ZHOU CUTS THE RIBBON OPENING A NEW STEEL MILL.

RELAXING AFTER A HARD DAY ON THE JOB.

was 45, still far less than Zhou's own sixty years. Yet Zhou set the pace, marching at the head of the column and carrying a fifteen-foot bamboo pole with a flag of "The Fourth Contingent of Government Workers." When they arrived, he ordered everyone, including his aide, to participate in the regular work schedule. For more than a week they were all to be ordinary workers building a dam.

The work was not easy for Zhou. A twenty-year-old injury crippled his right arm, forcing him to strain while carrying some of the larger rocks. When those around him saw the pearls of sweat dripping from his forehead, they advised him to rest. He would not hear it, any more than he would allow a personal physician to accompany him. He wanted no special treatment. If he fell sick, he said, the same doctor that treated the rest of the workers could take care of him.

Zhou did have some special treatment. Whereas everyone else at the end of the day had to head for a communal barracks to collapse and try to regain their strength for the next day, Zhou had a private shack. He used the privacy granted by his spartan quarters not to relax in peace, but to continue to work. After the general lights out, his room would still be lit as he read reports deep into the night. The habits of so many years' standing could not be easily broken.

Otherwise Zhou lived, ate, and worked like everyone else. At first the others tried to make considerations for his age and position. For example, without mechanization all the rocks, called "watermelons" and "cantaloupes" to differentiate them by size, had to be passed along by hand up to the embankment of the dam. Zhou's line at first moved very slowly, and passed only "cantaloupes." Zhou quickly changed this by urging his workmates to move faster and send bigger rocks. Before long, Zhou's line had its share of "watermelons" moving rapidly along.

An air of cameraderie grew on the work site, and the usual competitive banter soon followed. The young soldiers and workers who were devoting their spare time to the project began to tease the older men who had difficulty keeping up. At one point, seeing that the older men were breathing hard from the work, a young soldier suggested they join in on a song.

An old cadre replied, "Singing? I could have done that twenty years ago. Now I'm old and simply can't do it."

When Zhou heard this, he laughed and said, "Only twenty years ago you could sing and twenty years later you can't? Isn't that a bit depressing? Where's your enthusiasm?!" Then he turned to the others there and urged. "Let's pick up the Yanan spirit and sing."

Zhou led the singing, and the old cadre picked up the tune. Depression turned to enthusiasm, and the Fourth Brigade talked of piling up rocks so high that they would reach the clouds. Such was the inspiration of Zhou Enlai—and the spirit of the times, for this was the very height of the Great Leap Forward.


*"RAISE YOUR ENTHUSIASM..."*

In one sense the Great Leap Forward represented the logical culmination of all that had gone before. In 1949 China had been perhaps the poorest country in the world, with widespread political corruption and social misery. Less than a decade of Communist rule had changed that situation substantially. People for the first time had enough to eat, and did not have to fear for their next meal, or for their lives when they went out on the streets. Prostitution and drug addiction were eliminated. Production was reorganized and output increased. Steel came pouring out of the mills at four times the previous rate. On the farms similar changes took place, as more and more peasants joined together to form larger work units. One success led to another, and forward progress appeared unlimited. It was only logical to assume that that progress could be made in a great leap.

In another sense the Great Leap made a radical break with what had gone before, because it threw out the blueprints for the earlier success. Initially China imitated the Soviet Union, but the vast differences between the two countries caused profound problems to fester beneath the apparent success. In January 1956 Zhou Enlai sounded the alarm to intellectuals: "We must discard all servile thinking...must not run to the Soviet experts for every question, big and small." By May Mao himself was calling for a mass movement of intellectuals to study China's problems, make known

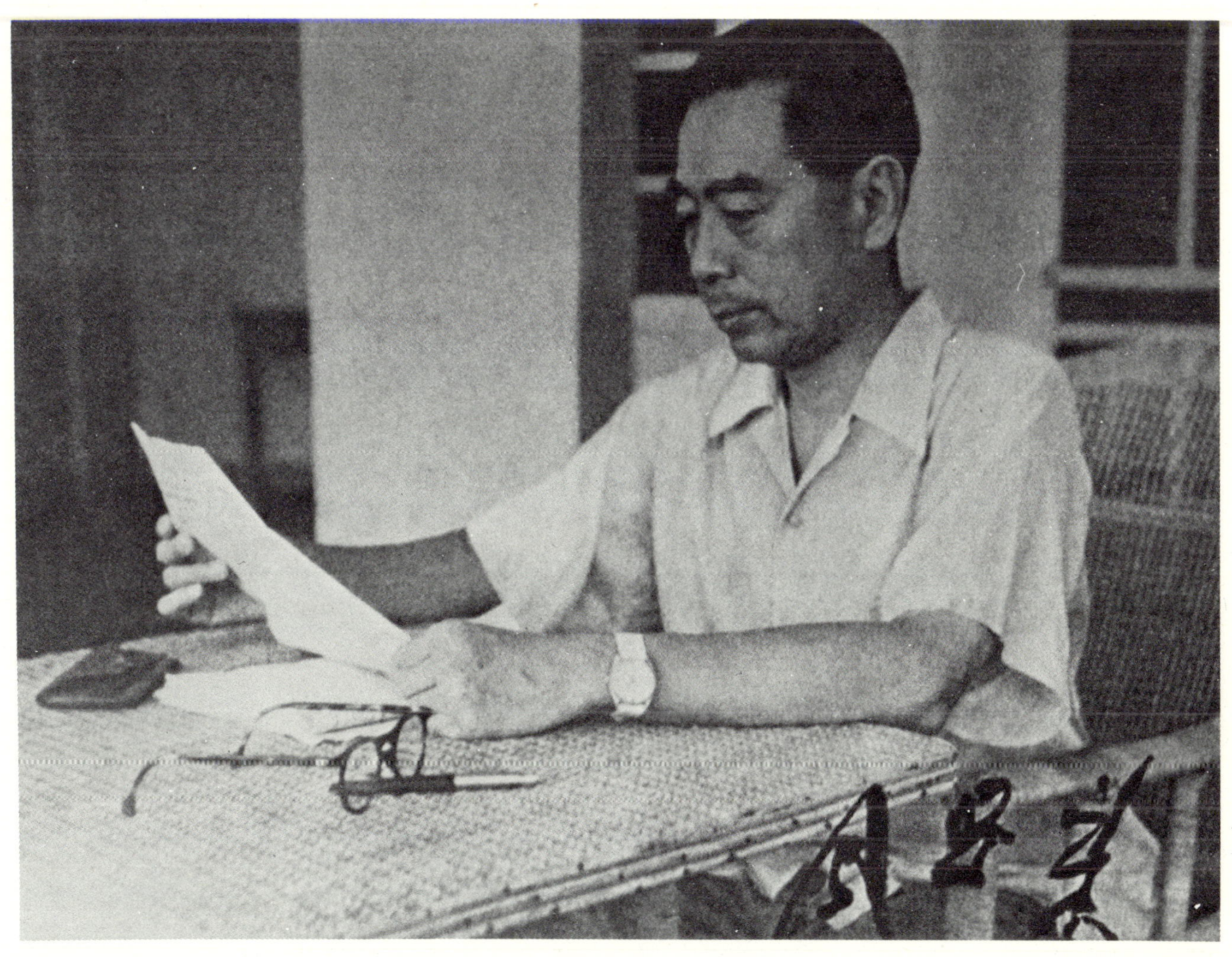

ZHOU REVIEWING REPORTS OF GREAT LEAP ADVANCES IN 1958.

ONE OF THE ACCOMPLISHMENTS OF THE GREAT LEAP FORWARD WAS THE "EAST WIND," A SIX-SEAT SEDAN THAT COULD GO 80 MILES PER HOUR AND GET 30 MILES PER GALLON. ALONG WITH THE WHITE-WALL TIRES CAME A RADIO AND HEATER.

MORE APPROPRIATE TO CHINESE NEEDS WAS THIS SMALL EXPERIMENTAL JITNEY, WHICH ZHOU TOOK FOR A TEST DRIVE.

THE GREAT LEAP, HOWEVER, WAS DOMINATED BY SMALL-SCALE RURAL PRODUCTION EFFORTS, SUCH AS THESE "BACKYARD STEEL FURNANCES."

**AMONG THE PEOPLE: ZHOU MEETS WITH CHINA'S BASKETBALL STARS.**

AMONG THE PEOPLE: ZHOU GIVES HIS AUTOGRAPH TO NATIONAL MINORITY STUDENTS VISITING BEIJING.

AMONG THE PEOPLE: URBAN YOUTHS ARE URGED TO SPEND TIME LIVING IN THE COUNTRYSIDE TO HELP BREAK DOWN THE URBAN-RURAL DIFFERENCES. HERE ZHOU CHATS WITH SOME "RUSTICATED" YOUTHS FROM SHANGHAI.

AMONG THE PEOPLE: THE TAI MINORITY OF SOUTHWESTERN CHINA HAVE A FESTIVAL IN WHICH THEY SPRINKLE WATER ON ONE ANOTHER FOR GOOD LUCK. ZHOU JOINED IN ON THE FESTIVITIES AND CAME OUT SOAKED.

AMONG THE PEOPLE: THE GREAT LEAP FORWARD PRODUCED INNUMERABLE "HEROES OF LABOR."
HERE ZHOU OFFERS A TOAST IN THEIR HONOR AT A 1959 BANQUET IN BEIJING.

their criticisms, and suggest ideas for improvement. Neither Zhou nor Mao at this point directly criticized the Soviet Union, but they were firm in the emphasis on self-reliance. Chinese had to think for themselves and solve their own problems.

Several years later Mao gave an example of the problem as it affected him: "I couldn't have eggs or chicken soup for three years, because an article appeared in the Soviet Union which said that one shouldn't eat them. Later they said that one could eat them. It didn't matter if the articles were correct or not, the Chinese listened all the same and respectfully obeyed. In short, the Soviet Union was tops.''

Far more severe, however, were the problems in the economy, which had made such substantial gains. According to a contemporary report, out of 800 employees in one factory, 126 were bosses or "administrative cadre." A country as poor as China could not afford one boss for every five workers. (Nor could the factory use them. The workers charged that they spent most of their time reading newspapers.) Yet even while the factories were filled with unproductive employees, unemployment was on the rise in the cities. Soviet-style development called for only the most modern type of factory, which absorbed huge chunks of capital but employed few workers. China, rich in labor and poor in capital, demanded just the reverse, factories where hard work could make up for limited resources. Similarly, the countryside experienced the problems of underemployment. Peasants overworked at planting and harvest time had little or no work during the rest of the year; so they would drift into the cities and aggravate the problem of unemployment there.

In 1956 and 1957 Mao Zedong wrote a series of articles proposing a new solution to these problems. Instead of the capital-intensive model based on heavy industry and favored by the Soviets, he advocated a more labor-intensive geared to medium and light industry. Such an approach allowed greater decentralization and prevented the formation of a technocratic elite. Mao's scheme for development, unlike that of the Soviets, discouraged any division between the cities and the countryside, industry and agriculture, or mental and manual labor.

While Mao wrote, the peasants acted. In Henan province near the Taihang mountains in central China, peasants continued to increase the size of their local production unit to the point where they could incorporate small industry and even organize a self-defense militia. Society and state fused in this new social unit which they thought should be called a "commune" after the famous Paris commune of 1871. In fact, they were still discussing the right name when Mao rushed down from Beijing to make a tour of inspection. After he examined their handiwork and judged the people's commune to be "a good thing," the Great Leap Forward was on.

In the next few months, communes were organized everywhere. Mao was ecstatic: "I have seen the great enthusiasm of the masses for socialism.... With this enthusiasm and party leadership, nothing is impossible.... The masses are the real heroes." Zhou responded, as we have seen, with direct participation in the movement, a major purpose of which was to tap underemployed labor for public-works projects. When asked to write a motto in his own calligraphy to be hung when the dam was finished, Zhou chose the main slogan of the day: "Raise your enthusiasm, Strive for the goal, Work more, faster, better, and economically to build socialism.''

Throughout 1958 people did work harder. An army of 100,000 volunteer laborers finished the massive Great Hall of the People in just a few months, working through the dead of winter. Major irrigation projects were started everywhere in the country, and a thousand new factories were built, in an economy that had seen the construction of less than 600 in the previous five years. New successes encouraged greater enthusiasm and brought the nation to a fever pitch. Many spoke of three years of hard work to be followed by a thousand years of communist utopia.

The bubble burst in 1959. Harvest declined, partly because of bad weather, partly because of damage done in the rush to produce the record harvest of 1958. New factories stood idle because of supply shortages which their builders failed to consider. Peasants even went hungry despite the bumper crop. Many had sold too much to the state before they realized that the actual crop might not live up to expectations. After everyone had feasted to celebrate the imminent arrival of plenty, they discovered that grain and livestock were in short supply.

Zhou Enlai had the difficult task of reporting on the accomplishments and failures. First in April, then in August, he addressed the government and delivered the message that, although much had been done, problems had arisen. "Because of lack of experience in assessing harvests under conditions of bumper crops, inadequate allocating of labor power . . . which led to rather hurried reaping and threshing, . . . the calculations were a bit high." But the basic ideas were sound and "part of the people's understanding how to transform China from a poor and blank country into an industrial state."

Other Communist leaders were not so sanguine about the results. Despite their own initial enthusiasm for the effort, they described the movement as "petty bourgeois" and "adventurist" and suggested that the theoretician behind it, Mao Zedong, was a "fanatic." Since the Great Leap had promoted the idea of a popular militia in place of a regular army, Defense Minister Peng Dehuai, responsible for the Chinese victories in Korea and for defense against the American threat on Taiwan, led the attack on policies which threatened to weaken defense industries. He was openly joined by Soviet Premier Khrushchev, who echoed Peng's complaints during a July speech in Poland, while in Russia *Pravda* lauded Peng. In August 1959, Mao and Peng finally clashed directly.

The beautiful mountain resort of Lushan in southeastern China was the site for three weeks of meetings between top party leaders who wrangled over the significance of the Great Leap. Peng Dehuai pushed his points, and strongly intimated what was already obvious, that he had Soviet support. Chen Yun, the fifth-ranking party member and a leading economic planner, supported Peng. Mao came under such heavy pressure that he could not sleep for three days, even after taking sleeping pills. But when the meetings were over and the dust had settled, Mao emerged the victor. Peng Dehuai was removed as defense minister and replaced by Lin Biao, a proponent of guerrilla war. The official position remained that already enunciated by Zhou: the Great Leap was basically a good idea that had run into problems. Even Mao recognized this. Speaking of supply shortages in industry, he said, "Coal and iron won't walk by themselves. . . . I had not thought of this."

After the Lushan meetings of 1959 the Great Leap continued, albeit with diminished enthusiasm and dimmer hopes. Zhou still made his visits to ordinary workers, but he could ill afford the time to stay and work with them. More and more of his energies were taken up by problems with the Russians.


*THE SINO-SOVIET SPLIT*

One of Zhou's first acts as foreign minister had been to sign a thirty-year treaty of friendship and alliance in Moscow; yet within five years strains began to show. In 1954 at Geneva, Zhou's run-in with Dulles captured the headlines, whereas a lesser incident went unreported but may have had greater portent.

The scene was a gala diplomatic reception hosted by the Soviet Union for China to which had been invited the ambassadors from Great Britain, Sweden, India, and other countries which had recognized the People's Republic. At the party Zhou moved from guest to guest, offering toasts and all the while speaking in English.

When he reached his Russian hosts, Anastas Mikoyan, the longtime Soviet Politburo member, snapped out in Russian, "Why don't you speak Russian, Zhou? You know it perfectly well."

Zhou retorted in English, "It's time for you to learn Chinese, Mikoyan."

"But Chinese is a very hard language."

"Don't worry. Come around to our embassy in the morning, and we'll give you lessons." Zhou then smiled and passed on.

The significance of this exchange was lost on the Western correspondents who overheard it, but afterwards the consequences of the Russians not "speaking" Chinese became manifest.

In 1956 the Russians did not understand the Chinese position on Stalin, whom Khrushchev had just denounced. The Chinese called for a more balanced evaluation, stressing both his accomplishments and failures. (Two decades later, Americans would not understand the Chinese assessment of Nixon after Watergate.)

In 1958 there was another communication fail-

AMONG THE PEOPLE: WITH MAO AND MEMBERS OF THE BEIJING MILITIA.

IN 1954 IN GENEVA, SOVIET FOREIGN MINISTER MOLOTOV WELCOMED ZHOU, AND
SINO-SOVIET FRIENDSHIP SEEMED UNBREAKABLE.

ONE OF THE SOVIET EXPERTS, A RETIRED ENGINEER WHO VOLUNTEERED TO HELP TRAIN CHINESE STUDENTS.

KHRUSHCHEV, LIU SHAOQI (THEN CHINA'S PRESIDENT), AND BREZHNEV IN MOSCOW IN 1960.

ZHOU LAYING A WREATH AT THE TOMB OF LENIN IN 1950.

REJECTED BY THE SOVIETS, ZHOU WAS WELCOMED IN THE THIRD WORLD. HERE AN INDIAN ON THE STREET CARRIES HIS PICTURE AND THE CHINESE FLAG.

IN CEYLON (NOW SRI LANKA), ZHOU MET WITH THE CHILDREN.

TANZANIA'S JULIUS NYRERE SHARES A JOKE WITH ZHOU.

ON A VISIT TO BURMA, ZHOU WEARS THEIR NATIVE COSTUME.

EGYPTIAN WORKERS GREET ZHOU ON HIS VISIT TO THEIR FACTORY.

ure, during the Taiwan crisis of that year. The Chinese held that their rights to Taiwan could not be limited or abrogated, and would not accept the American navy helping Chiang Kaishek's troops to hold islands just off China's shore. Khrushchev, more concerned with a general global conflict in which he would have to back down (as he did in the 1963 Cuban missile crisis) suggested that the islands be given up "temporarily." The failure to see the issue in the same terms heightened mutual mistrust, already strong because of Soviet criticism of Chinese economic policies.

In 1960 the divergent approaches came out in the open, during an exchange of polemics on "revisionism," and assumed the proportions of a formal split. The Soviet Union then attempted to pressure China by withdrawing technical advisors whom only a year before they had agreed to send. Zhou himself had gone to Moscow in 1959 to sign that agreement, and for this reason the split was something of a personal defeat. Perhaps this is why he minimized its significance in a 1960 interview with Edgar Snow.

Yet when differences of opinion could not be healed, once again it was Zhou Enlai who personally dramatized the new policy. In Moscow for the twenty-second congress of the Soviet Communist party, Zhou stalked out of the meeting when Khrushchev vilified Albania, China's only European ally. Two days later he spoke and made his own call for unity, arguing that fraternal parties and countries should not be criticized. The message fell on deaf ears. Zhou responded by laying wreaths on the tombs of Lenin and Stalin which described Stalin as "a great Marxist-Leninist," an obvious rebuff to Khrushchev. Zhou then left Moscow before the congress ended, and returned to a hero's welcome in Beijing. Khrushchev was infuriated, and assuaged his anger by moving Stalin's body to an obscure site under the Kremlin wall.

Zhou returned to Moscow in 1964 after Khrushchev had been deposed, but the breach was not healed. Since that day it has only worsened.

## A PERIOD OF WITHDRAWAL

The worsening Sino-Soviet split prompted new diplomatic initiatives. In December 1963 Zhou Enlai and Foreign Minister Chen Yi began a tour of ten African states and Albania which brought them into contact with leading political figures like Nasser of Egypt and Nkrumah of Ghana. Zhou used the opportunity also to get in a bit of people's diplomacy by visiting Egyptian factories and otherwise meeting with the masses. After their return and a brief rest, Zhou and Chen went on to tour Burma, Pakistan, and Ceylon. Their travels bettered diplomatic relations but achieved few concrete gains, and were soon overshadowed by the Cultural Revolution in China.

1966–1976

The rain came down without any letup, and the political organizers at Qinghua University were nervous. The rally they had planned for that day featured Zhou Enlai as a speaker. When they originally made their plans, they hoped for a sunny August day. Thousands of students would be attending the outdoor meeting, and no indoor facilities were large enough to hold the crowd. Now with the rain perhaps Zhou Enlai would not come.

A hurried call was made. "With the rain coming down this hard, should we delay the rally?"

Zhou's reply was firm. "Are the people there? Well, then, I'll be right over."

Zhou arrived soon afterwards as he promised, but the rally's sponsors were surprised to see him without an umbrella or raincoat. When offered some protection, he refused:

"Didn't you give me a Red Guard armband? You are being toughened by being out in the storm. I want to be toughened too."

The old revolutionary had not gone soft. Once again he was leading by example. The "Great Proletarian Cultural Revolution" was intended to toughen—literally, "steel and temper"—the youth of China, who had not undergone the sufferings of the old society or the rigors of the revolution. Zhou had undergone both, but still he joined in with the young Red Guards, most of whom were only a quarter of his age.

Thus the Cultural Revolution began in the summer of 1966. Millions of students flocked to Beijing, where they paraded before Mao Zedong and other leaders. Foot soldiers in an army recruited by Mao to combat bureaucratism and keep the revolution alive, they had little more than Mao's vague directive to "bombard the headquarters" to guide their actions. Nevertheless, they set out with determination and spirit to weed out "ghosts and monsters" and "those in authority taking the capitalist road."

Zhou's role was to keep China's ship of state afloat while it was buffeted by the waves of revolution, for the tempest would be severe. Up through August the party had generally agreed on the goals of the movement, which, like other movements in the past, was intended to reorganize the party by subjecting it to popular criticism. Then Mao put up a poster opening the highest levels of the party to scrutiny and criticism. This guaranteed disruption of the entire state apparatus. Zhou, dubbed China's "housekeeper" by Mao, had the task of preserving what order was possible.

Initially Zhou succeeded in preventing the students from interfering with production or causing other major dislocations, but very soon his job became like mopping up after the sorcerer's apprentice. After the administrator responsible for coal production was grilled for forty hours straight and then died of a heart attack, Zhou became "very upset," and let it be known. Nor did he approve of the humiliating treatment meted out to many old cadres who had devoted their lives to the revolution. Zhou did not believe that they should be marched through the streets with dunce caps in the same way that cruel and rapacious landlords had been a quarter century earlier.

Zhou reached his boiling point during the attack on Chen Yi, the foreign minister and Zhou's close personal friend. In August 1967 a large Red Guard meeting was held to criticize Chen Yi. Zhou came to defend his friend, but was not allowed to speak. Fortunately, the grizzled, plain-speaking veteran of many party battles needed no help in defending himself against his immature and inexperienced interrogators. But his proud and disdainful bearing angered his accusers, who became determined to convict him at any cost.

Two weeks later, a large party of Red Guards invaded government offices to search for incriminating evidence on Chen Yi. They found Zhou Enlai. This time Zhou was free to speak, and he spent eighteen hours, without food or rest, arguing with the Red Guards over foreign policy. They were clearly no match for Zhou, and some thought they should get back to Chen Yi. When word came that Chen Yi had been spotted in a car which could be intercepted and several Red Guards suggested doing just that, Zhou exploded:

"If anyone tries to intercept Chen Yi's car, I'll go right out there and pull him out. And if anyone wants to capture him at the Great Hall of the People, they'll have to climb over me first to get at him."

Seventy years old, he had lost none of his fire and he stopped these Red Guards in their tracks.

But the larger movement had degenerated into

THE ONLY UMBRELLA AVAILABLE THAT DAY AT QINGHUA UNIVERSITY WAS AT THE SPEAKER'S
PLATFORM, WHERE IT PROTECTED A BARE LIGHT BULB AND THE MICROPHONE. HERE ZHOU SPEAKS
WHILE STUDENTS STAND BY IN THE RAIN.

LEFT: ON AUGUST 18, 1966, ZHOU ADDRESSED NEARLY
A MILLION RED GUARDS GATHERED IN BEIJING
WHILE MAO LOOKED ON.

BELOW: ZHOU SITS WITH THE STUDENTS IN THE RAIN.

DURING THE CULTURAL REVOLUTION, ZHOU FREQUENTLY ADDRESSED AUDIENCES WHILE DRESSED IN AN ARMY UNIFORM WITH A RED GUARD ARMBAND. NEVERTHELESS, HE DID NOT ALWAYS HAVE THE SYMPATHY OF THE ARMY OR THE RED GUARDS.

ZHOU AND MAO SIT ON THE GROUND AT TIANANMEN TO WATCH THE NATIONAL DAY (OCTOBER 1) FIREWORKS IN 1966.

ONE OF THE FIRST PUBLIC SIGNS OF CHANGE IN SINO-AMERICAN RELATIONS CAME IN 1970, WHEN EDGAR SNOW WAS WELCOMED TO THE TIANANMEN ROSTRUM ON NATIONAL DAY.

chaos. Not content with attacking their own foreign minister, some of the more radical elements burned down the British embassy in Beijing. A month earlier, in July 1967, conflicting Red Guard factions nearly started a civil war in the central China city of Wuhan when the local military commander arrested representatives from Beijing. Zhou negotiated a solution to the Wuhan imbroglio, but arrived too late to prevent the embassy fire.

Mao Zedong had been away from Beijing touring the provinces. He came back praising the Cultural Revolution as "not just good but excellent." But the damage was there for all to see; so a new danger was discovered, the "ultra left." Extremism was to be brought under control, order was to be restored, and the army was to bear the burden of rule while the devastated party and army were rebuilt. Exactly thirteen months of "bombarding the headquarters" had ended.


### RETURN TO NORMALCY

The excesses of the Cultural Revolution left a legacy of bitterness and factionalism. The movement which had been aimed initially at a small handful had engulfed the entire society, fostering extremism and divisiveness. Schools were completely shut down. Many factories were disrupted.

Zhou attempted to minimize the damage: "Such a world-shaking revolutionary movement of course exacts a certain price.... We took account of this in advance." He expected that people could be brought together in the new revolutionary committees which were prescribed as an antidote for factionalism. As a conciliatory gesture, he dismissed any charges against the extremist youth who assaulted him, since they had "been led astray, deluded" by a "few wicked leaders."

Zhou turned his attention first to the foreign ministry, where the campaign against Chen Yi had been masterminded by Yao Dengshan, the former ambassador to Indonesia who had been roughed up by an anti-Chinese mob there, and who had used his prestige to seize de facto control of the ministry. Zhou had him arrested. The subsequent trial found him guilty, and he was sentenced to three years in jail. Chen Yi was restored to his rightful position, but cancer prevented him from playing a major role in the foreign policy developments before his death in 1973.

In his other efforts to restore the government and party structures, Zhou encountered opposition from Lin Biao and other leftist generals who opposed Zhou's restoration of bureaucrats disgraced during the Cultural Revolution. Because of the importance of the army for the restoration of order, as well as continuing strong animosity against many of the former officials, Lin held the upper hand until April 1969, when the ninth party congress officially named him Mao's successor. But the border conflict with the Soviet Union in that same month apparently turned the tide in favor of Zhou Enlai, who pressed for a more rapid return to normalcy to cope with the crisis. By late 1970, Zhou told Edgar Snow, 95 percent of the dismissed cadres had been reinstated.

During his struggle with Lin Biao, Zhou Enlai had another problem with which to contend, the reestablishment of Sino-American relations. After two decades of hostility, the American government began to sound a new note. In his 1969 inaugural address, President Nixon spoke of ending a "period of confrontation" and "entering an era of negotiations" in Sino-American relations. But Nixon's decision to invade Cambodia quickly chilled the potential thaw. Then in November 1970 President Yahya Khan of Pakistan personally presented Zhou Enlai with a private letter from Nixon inquiring about secret top-level negotiations. Zhou quickly conferred with Mao and then told the Pakistani president that a "high-level person" would be welcomed for face-to-face discussions. To cement this offer, Mao Zedong told Edgar Snow in December that he would be happy to talk with Nixon "either as a tourist or as president."

Initiative remained in American hands in early 1971, as Nixon reported to Congress in February that "the United States is prepared to see the People's Republic of China play a constructive role in the family of nations." He added that any "dialogue" could not be "at the expense of international order or our own commitments." Within weeks the meaning of this qualification became clear, when South Vietnamese forces crossed over

ZHOU STILL RETAINED A DEEP RESPECT FOR HIS "ELDER BROTHER" IN THE COMMUNIST MOVEMENT. HO CHI MINH. THE TWO ARE SEEN HERE EMBRACING DURING ZHOU'S 1960 VISIT TO VIETNAM.

ZHOU GREETS PRESIDENT NIXON AS HE DISEMBARKS FROM HIS PLANE.

HIS HANDSHAKE NO LONGER SPURNED, ZHOU SAYS GOODBYE AT THE SHANGHAI AIRPORT.

ZHOU ATTENDS TO KISSINGER'S NEEDS DURING A BEIJING BANQUET.

into Laos. Like the Cambodian invasion the year before, the Laotian incursion threatened to destroy any rapprochement.

Zhou Enlai rushed to Hanoi to deliver a warning like that he gave the United States before the Korean war. In a forceful address to a huge rally, he threatened, ''If U.S imperialism should obdurately go down the road of expanding its war of aggression in Indochina, the Chinese people will take all necessary measures, not flinching even from the greatest national sacrifices, to give all-out support and assistance.'' Washington received the message. The invading army was withdrawn and, though heavy bombing continued, American troops began to make their pullout from Indochina. The way was now clear for the ''high-level person'' to come to China.

On his way back to China from Hanoi, something strange happened to Zhou. His plane was forced down by Chinese military jets. When he came out of the plane, the highly indignant Zhou demanded an explanation from the obviously embarrassed commanding officer. Fortunately, the general was a quick-witted man, and emphasized that he had received orders to shoot down the ''enemy'' plane about to intrude into Chinese airspace. The general took it upon himself, when he realized that the plane was an unarmed passenger craft, to first force it down and then investigate. This decision saved Zhou's life. Mollified, Zhou accepted the general's explanation and thanked him. Zhou also took with him the telegram ordering the attack on his plane. It was signed by Lin Biao.

Back in Beijing, events proceeded apace. Just over a month after the Hanoi warning, Zhou warmly welcomed the American ping-pong team to China and spoke of ''friendly contacts between the people of the two countries.'' As ''ping-pong diplomacy'' took effect on the American public, Mao's interview with Edgar Snow was published in *Life* magazine. Change was in the air and widely welcomed. But the Nixon administration, unwilling to resume formal negotiations without guarantees, demanded that Henry Kissinger, the presidential assistant for national security affairs and Nixon's factotum, first engage in secret talks to plan any visit.

Pakistan again served as the covert conduit. It was there that Kissinger disappeared from the view of the press, ostensibly because of illness. In fact, he was whisked to Beijing for several days of intensive talks with Zhou Enlai. There the younger man, widely regarded as ''brilliant'' in many American circles, was overawed by the older diplomat's stamina and sensitivity. In several days of discussions, many lasting four and five hours, Zhou kept the negotiations on course and guided them to a successful conclusion. Four days after Kissinger left Beijing, on July 15, 1971, the United States and China simultaneously announced to a stunned world that ''President Nixon has accepted the invitation (to visit China) with pleasure.''

Several days after the historic announcement, Zhou met for four hours with young American scholars to explain the significance of the change. In reply to their questions, he told them that the ''new forces of your era'' had broken through the barriers erected in the 1950s. And if the contacts between the people of China and those of the United States were to grow, Zhou went on to explain, then the normalization of governmental relations was necessary, since, unfortunately, states did still exist. When asked about the sensitive question of Indochina, Zhou reaffirmed his support for the countries there ''in their war of resistance against U.S. aggression.'' To reassure further these antiwar activists, Zhou told them that the demand that the U.S. withdraw its troops was ''even stronger than the demand to restore relations between the Chinese and American people.'' The new policies pursued by Zhou were not intended to undermine China's longstanding revolutionary commitments.

Others in China, however, were not so sure about the direction of China's revolution under Zhou's leadership. The sullen Lin Biao and his family nursed a grudge against Zhou, whom they derisively called a ''mandarin.'' His efforts in restoring order had blocked Lin's advance. More importantly, Zhou had Mao's support. If events continued in their present course, the revolution, as Lin conceived it, was doomed.

Zhou must have been aware of Lin's feelings. He held the proof that could have condemned him, the telegram ordering the attack on Zhou's plane. Yet he held back, possibly feeling that the telegram was insufficient evidence. After all, there could

ZHOU TAKES A REST ON TIGER HEAD MOUNTAIN ON HIS 1973 VISIT TO DAZHAI VILLAGE.

have been a simple mistake, and since nothing had happened, Zhou could be accused of engaging in palace intrigue to remove his opponent. Instead, Zhou left the whole question of Lin Biao to Mao, who had by this time lost faith in his former ''comrade-in-arms.'' Then the crisis broke.

Doudou, Lin Biao's daughter, her face in tears, broke in on Zhou Enlai. Through her sobs she explained her father's plans to bomb Mao Zedong's train. She could not believe that anyone would harm her precious Chairman Mao, the man of whom her father had once said that ''Mao Zedong's thought must be implemented both when we understand it and when we temporarily may not understand it.'' She did not know that Mao and Lin were now locked in secret combat, and that Mao was touring the provinces trying to undermine support for Lin. If Mao succeeded, Lin and his ideas would be finished; so Lin decided on extraordinary measures while he still had the power to influence events. Zhou, however, understood all this and knew how to respond. He gave orders to protect Mao's train and to arrest Lin Biao.

Lin made an escape only minutes ahead of his pursuers. Zhou had ordered the airports closed, but Lin had a Trident jet waiting. With his wife and son and others involved in the plot, he forced his way past airport guards. A dramatic shoot-out followed as the plane prepared for takeoff. Again luck was with Lin. The Trident taxied down the runway before it could be stopped. Then mysteriously, in the middle of the night, the jet crashed in Outer Mongolia. Lin's career met a fiery end.

Zhou now had to pick up the pieces. Mao apparently was stunned by this unprecedented turn of events, and subsequently took a less active role in government, especially as his health began to worsen. This was a particularly delicate stage in foreign relations, and news of so dramatic a crisis could undermine much of the work already done. Zhou rapidly made a series of decisions. The October First celebrations, China's Fourth of July, were scaled down. Mao could not appear with Lin Biao as he had the previous May Day, and questions were bound to be asked. Moreover, the government had to be swept clean of Lin's supporters without delay, whether or not they were involved in the plotting. Very quietly, eleven of the twenty-one members of the party's political bureau were dismissed, and wholesale changes were made in the highest levels of the civilian and military administrations. No word of crisis leaked. On October 25, 1971, just six weeks after the aborted coup, the United Nations voted to admit the People's Republic of China. Four months later, President Nixon made his historic visit. Questions about Lin Biao were overshadowed by diplomatic developments.

China entered a new era with the Nixon visit. The communique released in Shanghai at the end of the visit restored the status quo ante: the United States once again recognized that Taiwan was properly a part of China and a question for the Chinese to resolve. With that problem agreed upon, the path was cleared for full normalization of relations, a process which required further negotiations. But at least the People's Republic was no longer shackled by the diplomatic convention, enforced by American power, that it was not the legal government of China.

As for Lin Biao, the news of his actions was released gradually, in a way that did not pose a threat to China's foreign relations. The underlying tensions in Chinese politics about the course of the revolution remained, but the threat posed by fears of governmental instability was diminished. Diplomatic normalcy was restored.


### ''MY MIND CAN BE USED''

Soon a more powerful and personal threat confronted Zhou. In 1972 cancer was discovered and diagnosed as incurable. Zhou was given little time to live. Rather than retire, he decided to work with renewed vigor. News of the illness was suppressed; as far as anyone else knew, he had a ''minor heart ailment,'' not uncommon for a 74-year-old man.

His continued vitality was noted during a 1973 visit to Dazhai, China's model agricultural settlement. He accompanied a delegation of Mexican dignitaries, entertaining them with animated and informed discussions while they toured the village and climbed to the peak of Tiger Head Mountain to gain a panoramic view. Deng Yingchao, his wife, jokingly suggested that he had become an official Dazhai guide. The Mexicans were impressed, and praised him for being as expert in agricultural

ZHOU TALKS WITH THE VILLAGERS OF DAZHAI DURING AN EARLIER VISIT.

LEFT: IN 1973 ZHOU STILL LOOKED VIGOROUS.

BELOW: IN 1974 HIS ILLNESS BEGAN TO SHOW.

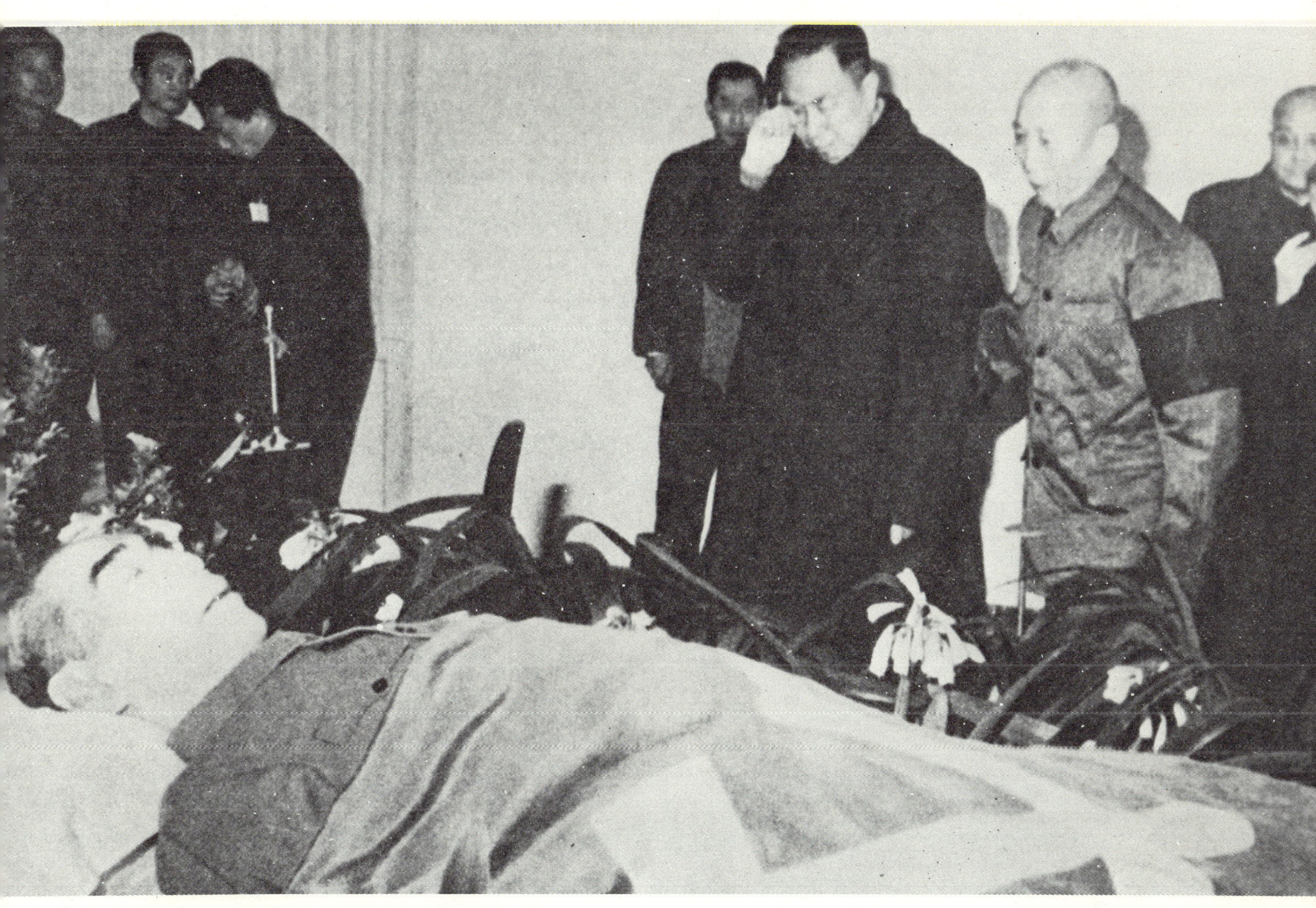

ZHOU'S DEATH BROUGHT GREAT SORROW TO THE CHINESE PEOPLE. HERE PREMIER HUA GUOFENG WIPES AWAY A TEAR OF GRIEF.

LEFT: BY 1975 ZHOU HAD AGED PERCEPTIBLY.

DENG XIAOPING (RIGHT), ZHOU'S SUCCESSOR, COMFORTS HIS WIDOW, DENG YINGCHAO, AT THE FUNERAL.

matters as in things political. Perhaps most amazed by Zhou's performance were two old peasants working by the side of the road. They saw Zhou climb and descend the high hills, and were very pleased when Zhou came over to talk to them. The conversation turned quickly to age.

"How old are you?"

"I'm sixty," said one.

"Seventy," replied the other.

"Then you are both my juniors."

They were taken aback. Leaders' exact ages were not commonly known, and after watching him they had thought Zhou was younger.

"Exactly how old are you, then?"

"Seventy-six *sui*," Zhou answered, using the lunar system favored by the farmers.

Age and death were very much on Zhou's mind that day as he continued on, paying calls on the oldest residents of the village and asking them their age. He was particularly pleased with an 86-year-old grandmother who ascribed her longevity to her dedication to the revolution.

Zhou knew such longevity would not be granted to him; so while he made his visit, he also prepared for the future by grooming a successor, the ever redoubtable Deng Xiaoping. Deng began his party career in Paris, where as a teenager he worked the mimeograph machine, grinding out the articles and manifestoes that Zhou wrote. By the 1950s he had advanced to the position of party general secretary, which made him a prime target of the Cultural Revolution. His defiant pragmatism, summarized in his retort to a question of ideological purity, "Black cat, white cat, it doesn't matter as long as it catches rats," inflamed the Red Guards and made him Number Two on their enemies list. But by the spring of 1973, Zhou felt he had learned a lesson and should be rehabilitated. In August 1973, at the tenth party congress, Zhou engineered his reentry into the political bureau, the highest organ of the party.

For Zhou all this was as it should have been. "Unity, criticism, unity" was a party watchword which had ensured a revolutionary regroupment after each factional struggle. This time, however, no new, higher unity was achieved. The opposing forces of the Cultural Revolution still nursed their grudges, and fought arcane struggles against Confucianism in which each side ascribed feudal ideas to the other. But while Zhou Enlai was still alive, this conflict was kept in check.

During 1974 Zhou's physical condition worsened, forcing him to spend more and more time in the hospital. In January 1975 he still had enough strength to attend the fourth national people's congress and deliver the main report, which summarized the gains of the previous 25 years and expressed the hope that China would become a "powerful modern socialist country." After that he was confined to bed, where he fought his final struggle.

At first Zhou received visitors and read reports in his hospital room, much as he had always done, except that he now needed longer periods to regain his energy. When this became impossible, he had reports read to him. He told his aide, "I can still hear; my mind can be used." Finally, he knew that the end had arrived. On January 7, 1976, he told his doctors, "Don't waste your time on me. The other sick comrades need your help more." The next morning, at 9:57 A.M. he died.

ZHOU ENLAI (1898-1976).

# EPILOGUE

After Zhou's death, China's pent-up factionalism broke out into the open. In April, the right wing tried to turn a massive demonstration of grief meant to mourn Zhou's passing into a rally against the leftists grouped around Mao. Fighting broke out, and the police were called in. Mao, then in the final stages of crippling Parkinson's Disease, attempted to resolve matters by elevating the centrist Hua Guofeng to the premiership. The unknown Hua had barely assumed power when Mao died in September, and factional struggle peaked in a preemptive coup by the right. The left-wing leaders, Mao's wife and three others, were arrested and vilified as the "Gang of Four." The right wing, under the leadership of Deng Xiaoping, who gradually replaced Hua as China's strongman, then proceeded to dismantle most of the Cultural Revolution's reforms.

How would Zhou have viewed these events and China today? Throughout his life Zhou advocated unity among the revolutionary forces. From Paris to Chongqing he eloquently argued that "Chinese don't fight Chinese." His moderating role in the Cultural Revolution stemmed from this very concern. He supported the political principles of the Red Guards, but not the excesses which those principles were used to justify. This moderation, however, has sometimes been interpreted as support for the right wing or for the unlimited power of the bureaucracy. But Zhou, who conceived of himself as an "ordinary party member" and an "ordinary worker," hardly ranks as a supporter of bureaucratic privilege. Zhou would not have approved of the restoration of bureaucracy at the expense of party unity.

And yet Zhou from his childhood was an ardent nationalist, aware of China's place in the world. "We should study for China to arise." The patriotism behind these words surges more strongly in China today than it did in the small Manchurian classroom more than half a century ago. Beneath the surface froth of factionalism the tide of change and modernization runs deep. The debate is about how to expedite this change, not about whether it is advisable. Certainly Zhou could only approve.

# SUGGESTIONS FOR FURTHER READING

A recent scholarly article published in England deplored the dearth of biographies of Zhou Enlai. At present there are only three others in English.

Kai-yu Hsu's *Chou En-lai: China's Gray Eminence* (New York, 1968), though completed a dozen years ago, still remains the standard scholarly work on Zhou's life. It did not have the benefit of recent Chinese sources, and had to rely on interviews with people who knew him.

John McCook Roots did know Zhou in the 1930s, and his book, *Chou: An Informal Biography of China's Legendary Chou En-lai*, adds his personal knowledge to Hsu's research and also brings the work more up to date.

Jules Archer's *Chou En-lai* (New York, 1972) tells Zhou's story in a lively manner without adding any new information.

Until the material recently published in China is translated, those who wish to know more about Zhou should turn to general accounts of Chinese history, since Zhou was a major shaper of modern China. A general text which can be highly recommended is *Mao's China: A History of the People's Republic* by Maurice Meisner (New York, 1977).

# ACKNOWLEDGMENTS

The author wishes to acknowledge the following for the use of their photos:

UPI, 2, 5, 24, 36, 37, 39, 41, 42, 64, 65, 66, 80, 106, 117, 120, 121, 140, 141, 161, 162

Robert Capa/Magnum, 75

Kelley & Walsh, 21, 22, 29, 30, 33, 34, 35, 38, 40, 44

Wide World Photos, 89, 93, 97

Center for Chinese Studies, 93

with special thanks going to NCNA and China Pictorial for the remaining photos.